HEAVEN
Close Encounters
of the God Kind

HEAVEN
Close Encounters
of the God Kind

by
Jesse Duplantis

JESSE DUPLANTIS MINISTRIES
Preaching the Gospel to the World

25th Printing 2010
HEAVEN – Close Encounters of the God Kind
ISBN 978-0-9743829-4-4
Copyright © 1988 by Jesse Duplantis
All Rights Reserved. Published 1996

Published by Jesse Duplantis Ministries
PO Box 1089
Destrehan, Louisiana 70047 USA
www.jdm.org

Jesse Duplantis Ministries is dedicated to reaching people and changing lives with the Gospel of Jesus Christ. For more information, or to purchase other products from Jesse Duplantis Ministries, please contact us at the address above.

Contents

Introduction

In this book I share some of the events that have happened to me personally in my relationship with God. I call them close encounters of the God kind. One of the events I share about in this book is my trip to heaven in 1988.

For a long time after it happened, I talked only a little about that trip until the Lord began releasing me to say some things. Sometimes people want to take an experience they hear like that and; because it's so glorious, so totally awesome; run with it — concentrate on it. I loved and enjoyed my trip to heaven and believe you'll be blessed reading about it. But what keeps us in relationship with the Lord is daily growing in the Word of God. Faith isn't created by hearing about an experience someone has had with God; **Faith cometh by hearing, and hearing *by the word of God*** (Romans 10:17).

From my trip, I understood heaven in a truly physical sense. It's a real place. I know that heaven is a fact. It's beyond a hope; to me it's the reality. But people don't have to believe me — the proof of what

I experienced is the fruit in the lives of the people who receive the message.

People have asked me, "Why did the Lord take you to heaven?" I didn't know. He could have taken one of *them*, and He may still — I'm not a unique individual by any means. But then one day it dawned on me why He took me to heaven — I do just love my Jehovah God! I'm willing to give Him anything I have, and I know He's willing to give me everything He has.

I'm a man who believes in taking steps by faith. I won't stay in the boat; I'm going to walk on that water! My feet may get wet and I might sink a few times, but I know that Jesus will always be out there on that water, and He always is. Before I go down, I grab for His feet. Then He picks me up, dries me off and sends me on across that sea. There's nothing we can't do through Christ Jesus. As God's Word says, **If thou canst believe, all things are possible to him that believeth** (Mark 9:23).

The description of heaven in this book is a prophecy. The Lord has wonderful things in store both on earth and in heaven for us — He blesses abundantly those who know, love and obey Him. He said, "Tell them I'm coming." He took me all the way to heaven to say that to me! I saw the great compassion Jesus has for those who haven't received Him as Savior. I came back more compelled than ever to tell people about Him!

As you read, judge this message for yourself. Does it witness with your spirit? Does it minister to you? Does it bring fruit into your life? If it does, then I know you will want to join me and *tell them He's coming*!

CHAPTER ONE

The First Close Encounter With God

I call the types of experiences I relate in this book *close encounters of the God kind*. When God gets close to you, your spirit will know it, your soul will know it and your body will know it!

In Genesis 1:26-28 let's look at what we might call the very *first* close encounter of the God kind.

And God said, Let us make man in our image, and after our likeness....

Genesis 1:26

Do you want to know what God looks like? He looks like you and me. We're made in His image.

People who hear me preach sometimes ask me, "Why do you act the way you do, Brother Jesse? You're so expressive!" I act that way because I'm made in God's likeness.

Let me tell you something about God: He isn't quiet. He's a noisy God. He's theatrical in the things He does. He expresses what He feels. Think about that. He is an all-consuming, powerful God.

So God said:

Let us make man in our image, after our likeness: and let them have dominion over the fish of the sea, and over the fowl of the air, and over the cattle, and over all the earth, and over every creeping thing that creepeth upon the earth.

So God created man in his own image, in the image of God created he him; male and female created he them.

And God blessed them, and God said unto them, Be fruitful, and multiply, and replenish the earth, and subdue it....

Genesis 1:26-28

It was odd to me that God would use a word like *subdue* in such a perfect society as was in the beginning. But God was hinting to Adam, letting him know what was to come. He was giving Adam a clue that, even in a perfect society, there would be things that got out of line. That's why God used such a strong Hebrew word, telling Adam to subdue the earth.

God was warning Adam about the snake that would come with its mouth open. He was hinting to Adam: "That snake will start talking to your wife and try to mess up everything that was created. You have to shut him up! You have dominion over everything I have created, so subdue it! Put it down!"

But Adam didn't do what God told him to do. He missed God's hint. He was thinking about being fruitful and multiplying and replenishing the earth. He forgot about subduing.

In a sense, the first close encounter of the God kind came through Adam. Notice God didn't curse Adam and his wife; He blessed them. Scripture says:

And God blessed them, and God said unto them, Be fruitful, and multiply, and replenish the earth, and subdue it... (v. 28).

Adam is the only man in the flesh who actually saw Jehovah God face to face and lived. Adam had in him Jehovah Himself. Adam had the very essence of Who God is. God was two inches from Adam's nose when He breathed life into him, and Adam became a living soul. The Bible says:

And the Lord God formed man of the dust of the ground, and breathed into his nostrils the breath of life; and man became a living soul.

Genesis 2:7

It wasn't like God gave Adam CPR to fill his lungs with oxygen. If God had done that, He would have held Adam by the nose and breathed into his mouth. But this Scripture says God breathed into Adam's *nostrils* the breath of life. After life had been breathed into Adam, he opened his eyes; then he saw the Creator.

That was the first close encounter of the God kind.

Adam's physical body was not created; his body was formed out of the dust of the ground. It was his soul, or his spirit, that was created. That's when God instilled life into man.

When someone dies, the opposite occurs. God is there to receive that breath of life back to Himself. When God breathes out, things come alive. When

He inhales, that life goes back into Him. Think about that.

When my mother died, I heard her breathe her last breath. God spoke to me then and said, "I just did to your mama the same thing I did to Adam." God had breathed life into my mother when she was coming into this earth. He then received that life-given breath back unto Himself as she was going out. That's a close encounter of the God kind.

If you go through the Bible, you'll find many of those encounters like with Noah, Abraham and Moses.

Jacob really had a close encounter of the God kind: Genesis 32:24 says that he wrestled all night long with **a Man** (as *The Amplified Bible* puts it). That Man was the angel of the Lord!

Gideon had a close encounter of the God kind. The angel of the Lord appeared to him and said, **The Lord is with thee, thou mighty man of valour....Go in this thy might, and thou shalt save Israel from the hand of the Midianites: have not I sent thee?** (Judges 6:12,14).

When he heard this, Gideon thought, *Who is he talking to? It can't be me. Why would the Lord choose me to do this? I'm just trying to beat out a living here on this thrashing floor. My family is poor, and I am the least in my father's house. I'm not a likely person for Him to pick!* (v. 15, author's paraphrase).

From his viewpoint, Gideon couldn't see why the Lord would pick him to do something great. Gideon didn't think he was capable of doing anything great. But the Lord's answer to Gideon was, **Surely I will be with thee, and thou shalt smite the Midianites as one man** (v. 16). Gideon obeyed the Lord's instructions, and the Lord caused Him to prevail over the Midianites!

God knows what we can do when He's behind us. He will lead us into victory as He did Gideon. What God is concerned about is whether we will listen to Him, trust and obey Him. In other words, He's interested in the relationship. He's hungry not only for relationship with us, but for fellowship. He wants to see us as much as we want to see Him.

You can have a close encounter of the God kind. You can start by talking to God through prayer. Prayer is the wing on which faith flies. Faith won't fly unless we pray. When that faith gets on those prayer wings, it will produce results.

In the following chapters I share some of the close encounters of the God kind that have happened to me through my life. My first experience occurred when I was just a boy....

"Fear God, Boy!"

There were four kids in my family, three boys and a girl. We three boys slept together in one room.

After my mother accepted Jesus as her Lord and Savior, she would come into our room at night while we were sleeping and pray for us, laying hands on us as she prayed. (Mama told me about this after I got saved.)

Called To Preach

One night before praying for us, Mama said, "Lord, I want a preacher. Which one will be my preacher?"

The Lord answered, "Jesse."

When Mama heard my name, she said, "What? No, not Jesse. It can't be Jesse — he's a heathen!" (Had I been awake and heard what she heard, I would have said, "Definitely not Jesse!")

As I was lying there in bed asleep, my mama laid her hands on me and said, "God, You're calling this boy. He may not realize it; but, Lord, wherever he goes, just follow him."

The laying on of hands is a powerful tool used in the Scriptures, and God honored His Word to my mother. I received an anointing that night without even knowing what had happened.

My First Encounter of the God Kind

I had my first encounter of the God kind when I was about nine years old. As a boy, I had no fear. I didn't fear anything — no matter what it was — nothing scared me. I didn't fear God because I didn't really know if He existed. I didn't understand Him. But that night I experienced some fear.

We were living in a mobile home at the time. After I got into bed, I experienced something like a dream, yet it wasn't a dream. It was more like a vision.

There was thundering and lightning; then I saw the face of a man with a gray beard coming toward me in the sky. He started hollering at me, saying, "Fear God, boy! Fear God!" As a nine-year-old, that really scared me!

I ran into my mother's room and said, "Mama, there was a man by my bed, and he told me to fear God!"

"What are you afraid of?" she asked me.

"He told me to fear God!"

"You need to respect God," she said.

My mother realized that I had experienced a close encounter of the God kind that night. It was the beginning, setting the pattern of what was going to happen later in my life. I will never forget it.

Confused About God

But I was confused about God. I didn't really understand Him and I was afraid of Him. I thought if He came to town He surely would kill me. I was scared, yet I was aware of His Spirit around me at all times. I could feel and sense the presence of God.

When I heard Mama say things like "God will bless you," I would say to her, "If God will bless you, then how come we're so broke? If God heals, how come you're so sick?"

She couldn't really answer those questions. Most of the people we knew who believed in healing were sick and those who believed in prosperity were busted. They were taught to give, but they didn't know how to receive.

I seemed to experience some close encounters of the God kind everywhere I would go as a small boy. I can remember walking down school halls feeling God's presence around me.

I will never forget one time when I told a teacher about it. I said, "The Lord follows me," but she just looked at me.

I said, "I'm not kidding you — He follows me. He's liable to come right through this door in a minute."

"Now what would make you believe that, Jesse?"

"It just happens to me," I said.

Of course, she didn't understand it. I didn't understand it either, but Mama understood it. She knew.

My Close Encounter With God in a Car Wreck

In 1967, when I was seventeen years of age, I wasn't close to God. I was rebelling and didn't really want to have anything to do with Him.

I had borrowed my girlfriend's car and was driving along when I experienced another close encounter of the God kind.

The day before my encounter, my mother had told me about a dream she had. She said I was standing on a beach with a tidal wave of the blood of Jesus flowing over me. She couldn't figure it out, but she knew it meant something.

I thought, *Oh, here she goes with that spiritual stuff again!* I said, "Mama, I don't want to hear about that."

The next day I was driving down the road the way most seventeen-year-old boys drive — too fast — when I pulled out into the left-hand lane to pass a car. I was driving in a rainstorm, but decided to pass anyway. You know how boys can be behind the wheel — like driving 65 mph in a 35-mph speed zone. I took a chance, and it was a close call.

I got up to about 68 mph to pass that car when, all of a sudden, my engine went dead. I guess water had drowned it out. I could see another car coming straight toward me, and I didn't know what to do. I hit the brakes. My car fishtailed and started swerving all over the road, barely missing the other car. I hit something, and all of a sudden, I started flying. I will never forget how it felt to lose control of the car.

God's Hand Protected Me

My car jumped a six-foot mailbox. I went completely over it — I saw it come under the car. Later the police said when I started to slide, the wheel hit a stone culvert. The impact threw the car up — I cleared the mailbox completely — then my car began to flip. It flipped three times, end over end, and things in the car began to break and crack.

As the car was flipping, I kept holding onto the steering wheel. Then it was like I felt something grab my shoulder, and it held me in the seat. The steering wheel broke in my hand; the car door flew open and a piece of jagged steel was coming at me. I felt as if I was inside an accordion.

With everything being thrown around, that sharp piece of steel could have gone through my side and punctured my lungs. I could have been killed. But I was being protected.

I thought, *Whoa! What's in here with me?* I didn't know it at the time, but later I realized that it was the hand of the Lord physically holding me down! His hand grabbed my shoulder and protected me. It was like everything stopped. I didn't see His hand, but I felt its pressure on my shoulder. It just held me down. Then it slowly came off of me. That was the first time God physically put His hand on me.

"Popcorn Came Flying Out of That Steering Wheel!"

Now it's an amazing thing the way God knows how to prove things. As the car flipped over, and the steering wheel broke in my hand, up out of that steering wheel, I saw popcorn coming! Then, *Bam!* That popcorn started hitting me! I said, "Ohhh, look at this popcorn," just flipping.

When I came to a stop, I tried to get out of the vehicle as best I could, but I was jammed inside it, hanging upside-down. Thank God there wasn't a fire during that wreck. I could have been burned alive!

People stopped to help.

The car had to be cut open with a welding torch before I could be pulled free from it. Then I was put into an ambulance and rushed to the hospital.

I kept hollering, "There was popcorn in there! Popcorn!" I said, "Listen! Somebody grabbed me! Somebody's hand was on my shoulder! I would have died otherwise. I was flying." They all thought I was in shock. They gave me four aspirins at the hospital.

My mom and dad were called from the hospital. When I got on the phone, I said, "Mama, I've been in this accident."

Amazingly, she had driven right by that accident, but she didn't know I was in the ambulance she saw going the other way. She had said to my dad, "There was a terrible accident. Let's pray to God no one died."

After finding out I was okay, she asked, "Did you feel anything in that car?"

I said, "Mama, popcorn came flying out of the steering wheel!"

That went right over her head, and she said, "Besides that."

"Mama, I felt like somebody had grabbed my shoulder."

Immediately she said, "That was the tidal wave of the blood covenant in the dream I had the other night! God was protecting you! He was holding you down in that car so you wouldn't die and go to hell! You had better thank God that I'm praying for you, boy!"

I came out of that experience with only one little cut over my eye and a cut on my hand that was maybe a half-inch long.

The next day the story about my accident made the front page of the local newspaper. The headline read, IMPOSSIBLE TO LIVE.

When my parents came to pick me up at the hospital, I said, "Daddy, the steering wheel broke in my hand and popcorn was flying all around."

But the doctor kept saying, "He's just in shock. There wasn't any popcorn."

I also told Daddy about feeling that I was being held down through the accident. Nobody believed that either, especially after I told them how popcorn was coming out of that steering wheel!

But It Really Happened!

The next day I was so sore I could hardly move, but I said, "Daddy, I want to go to the wrecking yard and see that car for myself." So we did.

I kept saying to him, "Everybody thinks I'm in shock, but I know what I saw: popcorn came flying out of that steering wheel!"

So Daddy took me to the wrecking yard. That car had to be picked up with a wench.

When we looked inside the car, there it was: popcorn was scattered all over the floor!

We figured out then what had happened.

A bag of popcorn was in the glove compartment. As the car was flipping over, it began to break up and split apart. At the same time that the steering wheel broke, the glove compartment flew open and the popcorn bag was thrown out, *Wham!* That's when I saw popcorn going everywhere. It registered so much in my mind that I knew what I was seeing. The popcorn in the car proved to people I wasn't in shock. I had told them about that hand grabbing me. It was real, too! I wasn't in shock!

That was another close encounter of the God kind in my life.

Feeling God's Presence

As I grew older, I couldn't seem to go anywhere without feeling God's presence. But I still got more and more into sin.

I had started playing in a rock band. I would be getting ready to play in nightclubs or rock concerts, and I could hear the Lord talking to me in my mind. I kept yelling out, "Leave me alone! Leave me alone!"

We might be smoking dope or snorting cocaine, and I just kept hearing God's voice. It was audible to me. Looking at my drummer, I would say, "Did you hear that?" But he hadn't heard a thing. Then I would scream out, "Man, God's in this place!" I just kept feeling God's presence.

People who heard me talking like that thought I was tripping out on drugs. But wherever I would go, it was the Spirit of God working on me. He was honoring my mama's voice as she prayed for me.

I was like a baby that was being lifted up and protected, with God saying, "He's Mine, and no devil in hell shall rob that child from Me." God kept bothering me, but I kept running from Him. I was refusing Him. Why? Because I was afraid.

Sometimes I would just stop right where I was and make a long-distance call to my mother. I would say to her, "Are you praying? Quit!" Then I would slam down the phone.

God was reaching out to me, but I was still trying to get away from Him.

At church whenever I went to confession, I never told my priest the truth. I wasn't about to tell him all the things that I really did. I had been up to so much in those days that he could still be there today listening to my confession!

Hearing God Holler

I will never forget one time when I was in Mexico. I was right in the middle of a nightclub, and sin was running rampant. I can't even mention all the things that were going on where we were.

But in that terrible place, I heard God hollering in an audible voice. He was saying, "Get out of here — now!"

I just stood up.

A guy with me said, "What's the matter?"

"God said for us to get out of here. I'm afraid He's going to kill us all, so let's get out of here!"

I left that place, went back to my hotel room and called my mama in Houma, Louisiana. When she answered, I said, "Mama?"

She said, "I was praying, and God told me you were in that nasty, disgusting-looking nightclub. I prayed for Him to tell you to get out of there! Did you hear Him?"

"Yes, Mama. God has spoken!"

Through the years of experiencing these close encounters of the God kind, I became more and more aware of God's presence. A real change was about to take place in my life.

CHAPTER THREE

Saved, Then Called To Preach

It was September of 1974, and I still didn't really know God. I knew about God in terms of religion, but I didn't know Him personally. I was as lost as a goose in the fog. Then I got saved.

At the time this happened to me, I was in a bathroom in a hotel in Boston, Massachusetts. Of all places to get saved: in a bathroom. Why a bathroom? Because God knew I wasn't going to church. God will always go wherever we are when we're ready to turn to Him.

I had been watching Billy Graham on television. When my wife told me that Billy Graham would be on TV preaching that night, I said, "I don't want to hear Billy Graham."

Cathy said, "Well, he's successful. He pulls more people into the stadium than you do."

I sat down on the floor saying, "To get this woman off my back, I'll just sit here for a minute or two and watch this thing."

Then all of a sudden he started ministering and said, "If you're in a hotel room today...." In his altar calls he says that and finishes with, "...or wherever you might be, write me and I'll send you the same literature that I give the people here. And go to church next Sunday." I immediately got up, went in the bathroom and gave my heart to the Lord. I was really being touched, and I didn't want Cathy to see me cry. It was the only place to be private in the hotel room.

After getting saved, I went back home to Louisiana. I had to submit to the authority of a pastor and become a part of a local church in order to learn about God. I knew God had placed me in the Body of Christ, and I made up my mind that I was going to be a good person. I would go to church and do all the things I was supposed to do. I just wanted to be one of God's helpers.

God breathed in me a spiritual hunger that was beyond human comprehension. I began reading the Bible, and I would read it out loud. I wanted my ears to hear what my mouth was saying. I didn't even care if I was reading it out loud in public. I wanted so much to be a witness for God.

Preaching on the Job

Then something happened while I was at my job. What I'm about to tell is mind-boggling, but it's the truth.

I worked for a truck line at the time. We were inside its office, which had no windows, when, all of a sudden, the lights went out. We were in pitch-black darkness and couldn't see a thing. I honestly believe God knocked out the electricity in that place. I will never forget it.

While in the dark, people kept saying to each other, "Don't walk around. You might fall down."

I had been trying to witness to my co-workers, but they didn't want to listen. Then it dawned on me: *I'm going to preach to these heathens from hell!* Though I was saved, I didn't have a lot of sense, but I had a lot of zeal!

I said to them, "Do you see this darkness? This is what you'll receive for eternity. You're going to hell if you don't meet Jesus Christ as your Lord. You'll go into a pit where the fire isn't quenched!"

I was really preaching away at them when the lights came back on. They all just looked at me. I didn't know what to do then. I was a baby Christian. But it really caused a ruckus.

Two of the girls I worked with at the time were living with men. As a result of what happened that day, they went home, ran those guys off and gave their lives to Jesus. It was wonderful!

I Wanted To See God

I had read in the Bible where God had shown Himself to people, so I decided I wanted to see the Lord.

I said, "Now, God, You showed Yourself to men like Adam, Abraham, Noah, Moses, Peter and Paul. Why won't You show Yourself to me? What's wrong? I'm just a Cajun from South Louisiana, but I would like to see You. You said You're no respecter of persons, but it looks like You are."

I was getting a little angry at God. I wasn't praying right because I was just a baby Christian, and I didn't have much sense spiritually. I was wearing those spiritual diapers and praying wrong, but God understands. I just wanted to touch God.

When my wife and I went to a revival, I had another close encounter with God that shook me to my shoes.

In the middle of the meeting I was called out by the minister. He said, "You, sir...come up here."

The first thought I had was: *Oh, God, what did I do wrong?* But I really didn't think I had done anything wrong.

He said, "I don't know who you are, sir, but the Lord tells me that you have been asking to see Him."

My antenna shot up!

Then he said, "The Lord told me to tell you that He shall grant you a visitation."

I thought to myself, *But I've been praying two years for this, and God hasn't heard a thing I've said.* This occurred in 1976 after I was saved in September of '74.

The minister said, "He's coming to see you. He shall come to you at night. You shall be in bed with your wife. She will be sleeping. She will not hear and will not wake up. But the Lord will come to see you."

I asked, "When?"

He said, "Quickly."

I knew that minister was a man of God, so I went home thinking it would happen that night. Cathy went on to bed, and I just stayed up. I waited all night, but nothing happened. God didn't come.

The next night He didn't come.

I stayed up for three or four nights in a row. Still nothing happened.

Two weeks passed, but God hadn't come to visit me.

As a baby Christian, that made me mad. I got aggravated and vexed! I thought, *That guy just missed it; God doesn't want to come and see me!*

I wanted to do something for God. People had always told me I needed to do things for God, but they never told me how. I needed to know how.

Then God Showed Up!

I usually go to bed later than Cathy, so it was about midnight when I went to bed. I prayed like I normally do, thanking God for the day, then I fell off to sleep.

What happened that night was another close encounter of the God kind. It was one of the most amazing things that has ever happened to me. I don't know whether I was in the body or out of the body.

All of a sudden I was wide awake. I keep a clock on the end table by our bed, so I looked and saw that it was three o'clock in the morning.

The wind began blowing in our room. At first I thought it was the air-conditioning unit. But then it got stronger, so strong in fact that the curtains started flying up over the rods.

When this happened, I was lying on my stomach. I could feel the wind blowing through my body. It was going out my eyes, under my fingernails and out the pores of my skin. I just lost all strength and felt pinned to my bed.

What's happening? I thought.

Then I heard a Voice speaking audibly, saying, "You asked to see Me; turn around!"

This was an awesome experience!

Still lying there, I said, "God!"

Twice more, He said to me, "You asked to see Me; turn around."

I didn't know what to do. I felt as if my flesh was jumping off my bone. It was such intense physical pressure. My body couldn't handle it. So I didn't move.

The first thing I thought was, *Cathy would look at Him. She'll do it!* She was still asleep, so I began to punch her with my elbow. I said, "Cathy, wake up! Don't you know God's in the room?" But she just wouldn't wake up.

The prophecy I had received was coming to pass that night.

After the Lord had spoken those words to me for the third time, I said, "God, forgive me for being so stupid. Forgive me. I prayed wrong."

I could have physically moved, yet I couldn't. It seemed as if I was pinned to the bed. It was so awesome. I was out of breath. I could still feel the wind blowing. I thought, *God is in this room!* But I didn't know what to do.

I kept hitting at Cathy, but she wouldn't wake up.

All of a sudden, everything quieted down. The curtains quit flying in the air. Immediately I turned around and looked.

Nothing was there!

Then I got really mad at myself. I said, "You stupid idiot! What's the matter with you? You asked to see God. Then when He comes to see you, you don't even turn around!"

I was aggravated, so I hit at Cathy again. This time she woke up and said, "What's the matter?"

"You just missed it!"

"What?" she asked.

"God was here in this very room, but you had to sleep. So just go on back to sleep!"

"What did He look like?" she asked.

"I...I...I didn't turn around!"

Better To Believe Without Seeing

I got out of bed then and headed toward the living room. That experience had made me hungry, so I went by way of the refrigerator and fixed a sandwich.

As I sat down on the couch eating it, I was feeling like an idiot. I said, "God, You came to me. I heard

You with my physical ears, and I didn't even turn around!"

He spoke these words to my spirit: "I'm glad you didn't. It's better that you not see Me and still believe."

I said, "But it's my heart's desire to see You."

He said, "But you wouldn't be able to handle My glory. You're living in a corruptible vessel, a body that will die."

"Is that why I was hurting?" I asked.

"That's why your flesh was hurting. Your flesh cannot handle the glory of Who I am," He said.

This is a true story. I knew then what God's Voice really sounds like. It was another close encounter of the God kind.

Called Into the Ministry

I spoke to my pastor about this experience, but he didn't really understand it. He said, "I don't know about that. I've never met anybody with that kind of encounter."

So I talked to a man whom I esteem highly in the faith. He's a precious man of God, the epitome of dignity, having ministered for fifty years.

After telling him about my experience, I said, "This really happened to me. What do you think? Why did it happen?"

He smiled, then tears came in his eyes. He said, "I don't know why it happened. But I know it's of the Lord. You're called to the ministry."

I said, "No, you don't understand. I can play music, but I'm not a minister."

"Well, that's what God is calling you to do. Because you aren't already one, He doesn't have to untrain you. He can just train you now."

As I mentioned before, an encounter with God does not create more faith in you. God's Word says, **Faith cometh by hearing, and hearing by the word of God** (Romans 10:17).

So God began to breathe these things into my life and I began to pray, saying, "God, I don't need to see You to believe You." I had been praying wrong, but God understood my babyness. I was growing in the Lord. I just wanted more of the Word of God. I wasn't interested in anything but hearing what God had to say. Wanting to know more, I began to really study and pray and give myself to the Lord.

Some people think I immediately went into the ministry, but I didn't. God doesn't put spiritual babies out on the field; they'll just get embarrassed when their "diapers" fall off of them.

I never thought I would be a preacher. I can honestly say like the Apostle Paul: God put me in the ministry. I didn't want to be a minister; I just wanted to attend church like everybody else.

When I went into the ministry, I would pray and the Lord would answer me. I can honestly say that the Lord has done everything I have prayed for. This isn't an overstatement. I pray according to the wisdom and the Word of God, and He has been so kind to me.

I heard someone make this statement: "I would rather wear out than rust out." So I began to preach.

In my first year of evangelism, I held fifty-one weeks of revivals, which wasn't easy to do. I had a family to support. I never thought God would have me preach that much. I was running constantly, preaching every day, sometimes twice a day, Sunday through Sunday. I would preach anywhere. I just wanted an opportunity to talk about Jesus.

I believe that if you really know God you'll have a close encounter, too. You'll get so close to Him that after a while, you'll begin to hear Him out of your spirit. You may even hear Him physically as He moves within you.

God Heard Me!

I realize that God is concerned about my life, even to the minutest details. One of the greatest miracles in my ministry occurred as a result of God hearing and responding to a simple statement that I had made.

While on a plane flying to Dallas to preach the gospel, I said to myself, *I need to get me a pocket knife so I can clean my fingernails while I'm traveling. What I really need is a case knife. Then I spoke those words out loud.*

When I had finished preaching that meeting, I was given the honorarium. I was about to leave when the business administrator walked up to me and said, "Oh, Brother Jesse, this was put in the offering, too."

In his hand was a case pocket knife!

I started to cry. I said, "This is a miracle!" I went into the pastor's office and just knelt down, saying,

"God, You gave me this pocket knife. It doesn't cost much money, maybe four or five dollars. I could have bought one!"

He said to me, "I know you could have."

"Then why did You do it, Lord?"

"I heard you say it on the plane."

"But I was just thinking out loud," I said.

"I was listening out loud," He said. "Do you like it? It came from a little boy who really loved it. He always cherished it. It was his greatest gift."

"God, if You'll show me who he is, I'll give it back to him and go buy me one."

He said, "No, then I would not be able to bless him."

"But, God, that's so minute — so tiny."

"I know," He said, "but I'm concerned about even the minute things."

God blessed me so much with that. Another close encounter of the God kind had been manifested to me.

Being God's Witness on an Airplane

I give God certain times of my day, praying in the Spirit. I love to pray in the Spirit. It's a blessing of God. I will even pray out loud on airplanes, too.

People who hear me think I'm from a foreign country. Some of them ask me so clearly and distinctly, "You...speak...English?" After I used my Cajun dialect, I could tell they were thinking, *No, he doesn't speak any English.*

But I would say, "Yes, I speak English."

"Oh," they would say, "then what language were you speaking before?"

"It was the language of the Holy Ghost."

One guy looked at me and said, "Huh? The only ghost I ever heard of was Casper, the friendly ghost!"

I said, "Well, today you have an opportunity to hear about Jesus Christ through the personage of the Spirit of God."

Some people look at me and say, "You're a preacher, aren't you?"

When I say yes, they want to ask about scandals in the church or controversial issues.

One time as I was reading my Bible, it was as if the Lord said, "The devil is just trying to aggravate you." Then I said, "Lord, I'm going to look for an opportunity to confuse the devil today, because he's the author of confusion."

Later while on a plane, a man looked at me and asked, "Are you a preacher?"

I said, "Yes, I am."

When I saw his expression, I thought, *Oh, here it comes. But I just smiled at him.*

He said, "Well, what do you think about preachers that commit adultery?"

"Why don't we talk about *your* sin first? Then we can talk about preachers' sins. Tell me, mister, have you ever committed adultery?"

Looking surprised, he said, "What?"

I said, "Have you ever committed adultery? Are you an adulterer? Come on, tell me!" I was saying it forcefully.

Now when I used the word *adultery*, everybody sitting around us in that plane got real quiet. They all wanted to know about that man.

He just couldn't answer me. He stammered, "Uh...."

Then his wife got into it. She spoke up and said to him, "Tell that man something!"

But he never answered me.

As they were getting off the plane, his wife was behind him, saying, "Well, tell me, did you do that? Did you?"

I loved it. It was a blessing of God. I could just hear the devil saying to his cohorts, "We sure messed up today!"

As I was putting on my coat, I thought, *One more for the Lord!*

We were in one of those wide-bodied jets. As everybody was getting their bags from the overhead bend, that guy walked off, but his wife was still chewing at him.

The people around who heard us talking were saying things like, "He did it. I know he did. I could tell. When you asked him that, I said to myself, 'He did it!'"

One woman was so mad she said, "If he were my husband, I'd leave him today!" People get stirred up when talking about adultery.

As I walked off the plane, I said, "Lord, we sure messed up the devil, didn't we?"

That was a close encounter. God was there with me on that airplane. It was wonderful!

CHAPTER FOUR

My Experience With Angels

There have been times when I have seen angels in the physical realm. These were more close encounters of the God kind and a real blessing of the Lord.

One Angel Came at Night

A number of years ago, I was preaching for a pastor in Jonesville, Louisiana. In those days during meetings, I stayed at the pastor's home, as visiting preachers always did.

At that time I had been having heavy chest pains and suffering from stress, but I hadn't told Cathy or anybody else. I just kept preaching non-stop and moving at a fast pace. (I'm still doing that even today.)

Before going to sleep at night, I always like to put Scriptures in my mind so that, instead of thinking on bad things, I will think on the Word. That night in Jonesville, I had read a couple of Scriptures and was about to close the Bible, turn off the light and go to sleep.

I happened to notice the clock and saw that it was just before midnight.

Whether or not you believe what happened next makes no difference; it still happened.

I looked up and saw standing at the foot of my bed the biggest character I had ever seen in my life. I hadn't heard anyone come into the room. He just stood there looking at me. It was an angel of the Lord!

He was huge. He looked about seven feet tall and had blond hair longer than mine. He glowed. It was such a shock to see him standing there, I could have blown a hole in the wall getting out if I could have made myself move.

He said, "I have been sent by the Lord. You are under much stress, and the Lord sent me to tell you to sleep."

I wasn't about to argue with a seven-foot, blond-headed angel! I just accepted those words as being from the Lord. Immediately he was gone.

I had been holding the Bible in my hand, so I just rested it on my chest and fell asleep. I average about four, five, maybe six hours of sleep a night. But that night I slept for twelve solid hours!

It was noon the next day when I woke up. I hadn't moved all night long. I was lying there in the same position as before with the Bible still resting on my chest. I felt like a million dollars!

When I saw the pastor, I said, "There was an angel of God in your house last night."

He said, "You know, my two dogs were going nuts. I didn't know what was going on. I did everything I could to shut them up."

"I didn't hear them barking," I said. "In fact, I didn't hear anything except that angel of the Lord."

"What did he look like?" he asked.

"He was a big man."

One particular thing I remember about him was that he didn't have any wings.

Angels in a Church Service

I have had many angels come when I have been preaching. At one particular church, they came in the middle of my sermon. There were maybe a hundred people there at the service.

As I was preaching, I turned toward the seats where the choir usually sits and saw that those seats were filled with angels! They looked like shafts of light.

I stopped preaching and just looked in that direction, forgetting about all the other people in church.

Then a lady sitting at the back of the church jumped to her feet and screamed, "I see them too!" Nobody else saw them.

They walked down out of the choir section and off the platform. One of them walked right by me and smiled at me. I could see his facial features, but I didn't notice hair color or eye color.

As they walked down through the church, everybody just fell to the floor under the power of God. *Boom!* I was the only person left standing. With nobody to talk to then, I just sat down.

About thirty minutes later, people began to get up off the floor and sit back down in the pews. I asked some of them, "Did you see them?"

They said, "We didn't see anything, but we felt something."

You don't have to believe this, but it's the truth. There were sinners in that building, and they were crawling to get out of that place. The pastor of that denominational church didn't believe in being slain in the Spirit. The people in his church didn't believe in anything like that. But he and his wife and kids fell down under God's power. Not one person was left standing.

Later, there was a man in the foyer who said, "I don't know what happened. I lost all strength and just crumbled to my knees. I couldn't even lift a finger."

Yes, God has angels. The Bible says, **Some have entertained angels unawares** (Hebrews 13:2).

These experiences with angels were more close encounters of the God kind.

CHAPTER FIVE

I Was Translated by God

I had gone to Monroe, Louisiana, to preach in a convention. Normally I fly to meetings, but this time I had driven.

During the convention there in Monroe, a man called me from Lafayette, Louisiana, and said, "Brother Jesse, my little girl has such a high fever right now. Her temperature is at 103 degrees. We haven't been able to get her fever down. On your way home would you please stop and pray for her?"

I said, "Yes, sir, I'll pray."

I seldom go to pray for people in hospitals simply because I'm an evangelist. I don't cross the office of a pastor. Now don't misunderstand me. I will if the pastor asks me to, but that's pastoral care. I am very regimented to stay within my office. I know what God has called me to do.

Before leaving for home, I stopped by the office of a friend there in Monroe. He had asked me to stop on my way out of town, so that he could talk with me. We shared together for a few minutes.

Then I left his office at 10:35 that morning. I was headed out of Monroe, a town in northeast Louisiana, toward my hometown of Houma, Louisiana, in the southeast part of the state. I was traveling on Highway 165 going southward toward Alexandria, where I would connect with Interstate 49.

A Bubble Burst Inside Me!

As I was driving along, the Spirit of God began to bubble up inside me. I use the word *bubble*, because it was like bubbles were popping inside me. I was alone in the car.

Some people are not going to believe this experience, but that's all right. You'll never get a ride like this if you don't believe it can happen.

On Highway 165, there is an overpass that goes from four lanes down to two. As I went up the overpass, it was as if that bubble began to burst in me. I just felt like praising God, so I lifted my hand

and began to praise Him. I said, "Oh, Father, I just thank You. I love You, Jesus. You're such a blessing!"

Then it began getting stronger and stronger. When that happens, usually I get louder and start hollering, "Glory to God!"

Now what I'm about to write is going to blow some people's socks off. A close encounter of the God kind was about ready to take place. God didn't tell me anything, so I wasn't expecting this to happen.

As I was praising God, the car seemed to fill up with smoke. I thought for a minute that my car was on fire. But it wasn't like smoke I could smell. It was more like a fog. The anointing of God was flowing, so I just kept saying, "Glory to God! Thank You, Jesus!"

I don't know what happened next, but all of a sudden I was in the Spirit. I didn't feel or see anything. I was just in that fog, with smoke inside my car.

I was praising God and shouting, "Glory to God! Hosanna in the highest!" I was really enjoying myself, just worshipping the Lord. My natural mind was not registering anymore in the car. I was caught up in the Spirit.

"My Baby's Dying!"

When I came to myself, I was on the freeway in Lafayette, Louisiana. I realized then that both my hands were raised in the air. I thought, *Jesse, what are you doing? You can worship God, but you'll kill yourself in the middle of this worship. Fool, put your hand back on the wheel!* So I did.

I looked around, wondering, *What's happening here?* I was confused.

Then I looked at my watch. As I mentioned, I had left my friend's office in Monroe at 10:35. According to my watch, it was now 11:05!

I thought, *Something's wrong with this watch. It must have stopped. I don't remember driving all the way through Alexandria.*

The next thought I had was, *If I'm in Lafayette, I had better call that brother. I told him I would stop and pray for his baby.*

I stopped at a convenience store to use the phone. I called his house, but he wasn't there.

Then I thought, *Maybe they're at the hospital.* So I tried the hospital number. I asked to speak to that brother and was put through to their room.

When the receiver was picked up, I could hear screaming and hollering. I kept saying, "Hello? Hello?"

Finally a man said, "Hello?"

I said, "This is Brother Jesse."

Then I heard the voice of the baby's father. He said, "Brother Jesse, my baby's dying! My baby's dying!"

I said, "Whoa....wait!" I tried to carry on some kind of conversation to get some information, but I could hear doctors in the background saying, "Do something! Do something!" I didn't know it then, but the baby had gone into convulsions with a fever of 107 degrees! The doctors were working to save the life of that three-year-old little girl.

Then Came God's Healing Power

The father kept saying, "My baby's dying!"

Finally I had to scream into the phone. I said, "Brother, listen to me! Listen to me! Put your hand on that baby!"

He said, "Okay!" So he put his hand on her.

Then I said, "You demon devil from hell, I bind you in the power of Jesus' name! You'll not touch this baby anymore because God has spoken it from His throne!"

All of a sudden, after the screaming and shouting and hollering, I heard the father saying, "Praise God! Praise God!"

I said, "What's happening? What's going on? Hello?" I was trying to get some information. But everything had stopped.

Then I heard the doctor saying, "Look at this!"

That little girl had immediately stopped convulsing!

She opened her eyes and said to her mother, "I'm hungry."

The daddy was crying. The mother was crying. Then I started crying.

I said, "Well, how is she?"

Immediately the temperature had gone down from 107 degrees to normal!

He said, "Brother Jesse, I want to thank you! God healed my baby!"

I said, "Praise God, brother!"

I Had Been Translated!

Then I started thinking about my trip, trying to figure out what happened. There I was in Lafayette! You can't get from Monroe, Louisiana, to Lafayette, Louisiana, in only thirty minutes. It can hardly be done by jet, much less by car.

"Listen, brother," I said, "I'll see you later. I've got to go."

He was crying, "Thank you, Brother Jesse!" (I found out afterward that he checked his little girl out of the hospital two hours later.)

Then it began to register on me what had happened, so I called my wife. I had talked with her right before I left my friend's office in Monroe. This time she said to me, "Hey, where are you?"

"Cathy, I'm at a pay phone in Lafayette. Look at your watch."

Then she said, "You really made good time, honey. Well, hurry on home."

I wanted to scream, "Listen, woman, and hear what I'm saying!" Then I wanted God to zap me again, so that before she could even hang up the phone, I would be home. (But He didn't do it!)

When it dawned on me that I had been translated, I thought, *If I've been translated, then I didn't burn any gas.* When I turned on the ignition switch, I watched as the fuel gauge went all the way to full! I just cried out, "Oh, God!"

He said, "I had to get you to Lafayette in a hurry. That baby was dying." Why I had to be in Lafayette to minister to that family over the phone when I could have ministered over the phone from anywhere, I don't know. That's just the way it happened.

Now this is the stupid part of my story. I drove out onto the freeway there in Lafayette. I saw the state trooper office at the side of the road, so I pulled over. As I was sitting there, I started praying for God to do it all again. I said, "I know You can take me from Lafayette to home, God. Come on. Please...please."

I prayed. I stomped. I screamed. I hollered. But I stayed right there in that parking lot.

Then a man came over to my car and asked, "Can I help you?"

"I'm praying for God to take me home," I said.

I could almost see into the man's mind, as if he were saying, "Drive the car, you fool! Then you'll get home."

It took me two hours and fifteen minutes to drive from Lafayette, Louisiana, to my home.

Then it dawned on me that God didn't just fly me around for the fun of it. He wasn't just saying, "Let's go for a ride." He was working in the time of that emergency.

It was another close encounter of the God kind.

CHAPTER SIX

My Trip to Heaven

In August of 1988, I was preaching a revival meeting at Magnolia Christian Center, a wonderful church pastored by Paul Troquil in Magnolia, Arkansas. I was staying at the Best Western Motel there in Magnolia.

One morning the pastor called to say he would pick me up around noon and we would have some lunch. When I got up that morning, I knew something unusual was going on. I could feel a disturbance, an unrest, in my spirit. In the natural, it was a feeling of nervousness, with Adrenalin flowing, but for no apparent reason. I had no inclination of what was about to happen. But I can always sense when God is about to do something with me.

The pastor picked me up at the motel and we went across the street to a steak house. After we had ordered lunch, I felt compelled to go back to my motel room. I sensed an urgency.

Immediately I said to the pastor, "I don't mean to be rude, but I have to go back to the motel. Something is up. I just don't know what."

He asked, "Is something wrong? Are you sick?"

"No, nothing is wrong. I just have this compulsion to get back to my room. I'm sorry. Please excuse me."

I got up, walked out of the restaurant and crossed the street to the motel.

When I got back to my room, I hung a "Do Not Disturb" sign on the door knob and closed the door. I looked at the digital clock. It was one minute before one o'clock.

I had no idea what was going on, so I was ready to pray and allow the Holy Spirit to make intercession.

I thought to myself, *Maybe He wants to talk to me about tonight's service.*

I pulled off my coat and knelt down beside the bed. As I did, the digital clock flipped over to show exactly one o'clock. I said, "God, what's the matter? What's wrong? What's happening? What?"

An Appointment With God

Suddenly I felt a suction as if I was being pulled up out of the room. But I didn't look back to see myself leaving my physical body, as some people have described. I heard a sound, *Whoosh!* And I *was* pulled up out of the room! I gasped, "Aaah...." I don't know whether I was in my body or out of my body.

I did know I had left that room and I was zooming along at a phenomenal rate of speed, being carried in something like a cable car. It was a chariot without a horse, but not like one of those chariots we see in the movies — I was completely closed in. I could see through the windows that the chariot was racing along, but I had no idea how it was being operated.

Then I looked up. There stood another being. I realized that it was the blond-headed angel who had visited me in the bedroom that night in Jonesville, Louisiana. I asked, "Where are we going?"

He smiled and said, "You have an appointment with the Lord God Jehovah."

I felt the chariot slowing down; then it came to a stop. When the door opened, I experienced the shock of my life: I was in heaven!

It Was a Gorgeous Place!

Heaven must not be too far away. It didn't seem as if I had gone out of our galaxy. Of course, I'm not an astronomer, so I really don't know for sure.

As I stepped out of the chariot, everything I saw was so beautiful. I had always thought that when I went to heaven I would see only a city. But the first place I saw was Paradise; it hadn't been destroyed. Paradise is a big place, completely surrounding the Holy City. It is like being on another planet.

I fell down on the ground and began praising God, saying, "Glory to God!" The angel also fell down, saying, "The Most High God Jehovah! Hosanna in the highest!" Together we just worshipped God.

I was so excited. I kept asking that angel, "Where am I? What am I doing here?"

He said, "You have an appointment with the great God Jehovah. We must go to the city. You shall soon find out."

As I stood to my feet, I saw light that I had never seen before in my life.

Looking around me, I realized that God has with Him in heaven some of the things He created on the earth. I was surrounded by lush, gorgeous valleys, lots of mountains and streams of water. I even saw snow, yet it wasn't cold. I was amazed.

There were flowers in heaven that I have never seen before in my life and fragrances I have never smelled. I have never seen colors quite like those I saw there, either. There were reds, greens, purples, blues, yellows. The gold looked gold, yet it was transparent like crystal.

It was a beautiful land. Trees were lined up alongside the River of Life as it flowed throughout Paradise. Thousands of people were standing around under the trees. They all had been brought there in those chariot-like vehicles, the same as I was.

I had always thought that everybody who went to heaven was grown up. But I saw children too. I also noticed horses, dogs and large cats like lions.

Everybody seemed headed toward God's Throne in the Holy City, which I could see way off in the distance. His Throne was high and lifted up, and it could be seen from every direction.

The Clothing They Wore

I was still dressed in my regular clothes, jeans and a shirt, but I noticed that many people coming from those vehicles were wearing beautiful, glorious robes. When they stepped out of the chariots, they ran straight toward the Holy City — they immediately took off for the Throne — shouting and praising God.

Then I saw other people who didn't have on robes; they were wearing gowns. They started walking toward the city, but they seemed to get weak. I saw them walk over to the trees, pick what looked like fruit and eat it. Then they took some leaves off those trees, put the leaves up to their faces and breathed in, smelling them.

I asked the angel, "What's happening?"

He said, "Some of them have not lived the life they should. They believe in God and love Jesus, but they didn't live to their fullest potential."

Then I asked, "Will they still be able to go before God's Throne?"

"Yes, God is merciful to them," he said. "But they have to be prepared to stand in the presence of the Almighty."

"What happens when they eat enough of that fruit?"

"They will be strengthened," he said. "As we get closer to the city, the anointing and the light will get stronger. When we go before the Throne, it can be blinding."

Then I saw a man step out of a chariot like mine. He was wearing a gown, not a robe. He said, "I didn't think I was going to make it, but I did!" Then he fell on his face and kissed the ground.

The angel who brought him picked him up and said, "Come, come, my son." Then he took that man over to those trees and said, "Eat of this fruit and smell these leaves." I realized that those leaves were for the healing of the nations that the Apostle John spoke of in Revelation 22:1,2.

And he shewed me *a pure river of water of life, clear as crystal, proceeding out of the throne of God and of the Lamb.*

In the midst of the street of it, and on either side of the river, was there the tree of life, which bare twelve manner of fruits, and yielded her fruit every month: *and the leaves*

of the tree were for the healing of the nations.

I could see that the fruit helped those people to stay in God's glory.

I asked the angel with me, "Will he ever make it to the Throne?"

"He barely made it in, but our great God is merciful!" he said.

I knew Scripture that said to be absent from the body is to be present with the Lord. (2 Corinthians 5:8.) I thought that would happen the minute we passed over to the other side. Although some people don't live for God the way they should, God is merciful. He still helps them and touches them. But they have to be taught. What they don't learn on earth, they will have to learn there.

Those gowns were beautiful. After I had visited heaven, I began to do some research about the clothing I had seen. I found in Isaiah 61:10,11 (AMP) that God gives a robe of righteousness and a garment of salvation. There's a difference between the two. Look at Isaiah's explanation:

I will greatly rejoice in the Lord, my soul will exult in my God; *for He has clothed me* *with the garments of salvation, He has covered me with the robe of righteousness, as a bridegroom decks himself with a garland, and as a bride adorns herself with her jewels.*

For as [surely as] the earth brings forth its shoots, and as a garden causes what is sown in it to spring forth, *so [surely] the Lord God will cause rightness and justice and praise to spring forth before all nations [through the self-fulfilling power of His word].*

Some people don't live close to God the way they should. They know Jesus as their Savior, but they could do so much better. In heaven they will eventually be able to go to God's Throne, but it takes more time for them. Paul teaches that once we are saved we are to become examples of the righteousness of God. Consider Paul's teaching in 2 Corinthians 5:20,21 (AMP):

So we are Christ's ambassadors, God making His appeal as it were through us. We [as Christ's personal representatives] *beg you for His sake to lay hold of the divine favor [now offered you] and be reconciled to God.*

For our sake He made Christ [virtually] to be sin Who knew no sin, *so that in and through Him we might become [endued with, viewed as being in, and examples of] the righteousness of God [what we ought to be, approved and acceptable and in right relationship with Him, by His goodness].*

When I began to feel weak, the angel walked over to one of those trees, picked some of its fruit and brought it back to me. I don't know what kind of fruit it was, but it wasn't an apple. It was juicy and copper-colored fruit.

The angel said to me, "Eat this fruit so you will be able to withstand the glory of God." So I ate it, and I was strengthened.

As I was looking around, I wanted to see everything. I was like an eagle on top of a mountain peak trying to see everything down to the most minute blade of grass. I didn't want to miss anything. I had always thought that Paradise had gone away, but God took it to heaven and kept it there for us.

Then I Met Abraham!

The angel asked, "Are you thirsty?"

I said, "Yes."

"I shall get you something to drink," he replied.

There was a big, barrel-chested man across the river. He said, "I shall bring it to him." I saw that he had a gold goblet in his hand. He reached down and dipped it into the river. That river didn't look as big as the Mississippi River — it was more like a bayou or a big stream, a creek — only it was pure and clear.

I noticed the man's large size. He seemed of great age, yet he was young looking. There were no wrinkles in his face. It was obvious he was a patriarch. When I saw him, I knew in my spirit who he was and thought, *That is Abraham and I'm the seed of Abraham. This is my great-great-great-grandpa. If it weren't for him, I wouldn't be here.*

Paul taught in Galatians 3:14 that the blessing given to Abraham was made available to us (the Gentiles) through Jesus that we might receive the promise of the Spirit through faith. And our relationship to Abraham as his seed is explained in Galatians 3:26-29 (NIV):

You are all sons of God through faith in Christ Jesus, for all of you who were baptized into Christ have clothed yourselves

with Christ. There is neither Jew nor Greek, slave nor free, male nor female, for you are all one in Christ Jesus. *If you belong to Christ, then you are Abraham's seed, and heirs according to the promise.*

I watched as Abraham walked over to us. He gave the goblet to me and said, "Hey, Jesse! Drink this." I couldn't keep my eyes off of him.

To be sure, I asked, "Who are you?"

He said, "I'm Abraham. Paradise is my place."

I felt I knew him like my own father. I fell down on my face before him; but he said, "Stand to your feet. The only One you worship is the Lord God. I'm a servant. I have come to help you. I meet all the people who come here because Paradise is my bosom." When I stood to my feet, Abraham said, "I shall help you." Then he asked me how I was.

I said, "I'm fine, Glory to God."

When I said that, Abraham said, "Glory to God!"

Then the angel said, "Glory to God!"

It started a chain reaction as other people near us stopped and praised God. The sound of their praises seemed to ripple through Paradise.

He said, "Drink this water. It shall help you." So I did. It was so cool and refreshing; and it was being served to me in a gold goblet. I was impressed it wasn't a little plastic cup.

Then he told the angel, "Take him. He must stand before the Most High God."

But I wanted to talk to Abraham some more. My favorite Scripture in the Bible is Romans 4:17, which, speaking of Abraham, says, he **calleth those things which be not as though they were.** Like Abraham, I wanted to consider not, to stagger not and to be fully persuaded. (See Romans 4:19-21.)

Abraham said to me, "I'll see you again. I have to meet the others who have come to this land of blessedness."

The angel said, "We must take you to the city where you have an appointment." Then we got in line with all those other people and started going toward the city.

The Flowers Couldn't Be Crushed!

As we walked along, we came to a path of flowers. Their fragrance and beauty were beyond human reasoning. At first, I didn't want to step on them, but the angel said, "Walk on them." So I did.

I was amazed that the flowers were not crushed as we stepped on them, but I realized there is no death in heaven. Instead, each blossom popped back up and seemed to turn towards us as we passed so that we could always see their beauty. I noticed there were no brown leaves on any plants. And there is no dust in heaven. Nothing breaks down or corrupts there.

There Were No Shadows in Heaven!

Walking along with the angel, I noticed that I didn't cast a shadow. I kept looking down, so he asked, "What are you looking for?"

"I don't have a shadow."

"In this place," he said, "there is no darkness. God is Light in Whom there is no darkness, no shadow of turning."

The angel wasn't quoting Scriptures to me, but I knew that what he was saying was in the Bible. First John 1:5 says, **God is light, and in him is no darkness at all.** James 1:17 (NIV) explains that every perfect gift comes down from the Father of lights, Who does not change like shifting shadows.

I said, "Wait a minute; let me see if I can make a shadow."

"I told you there is no darkness. This is a place of light — *all* light. God encompasseth all."

I looked on mountains. I looked in streams. I looked in all kinds of places trying to find a shadow. But I could find no darkness at all. Everything was light. The light was phenomenal, beyond human reasoning.

The Fragrance I Smelled

There was a fragrance in the air, so I asked the angel, "What's that smell?"

He said, "It's the fragrance of God. He's in everything here." I believe he meant the fragrance was all through heaven.

Again, I fell down on my face and started worshipping God. I said, "The great God Jehovah!" Then the angel said, "Hosanna in the highest!"

CHAPTER SEVEN

I Saw Kids in Heaven With Jesus

All of a sudden, I heard kids singing and praising God. Then I saw them. They were carrying little harps.

I thought, *Now what are these kids doing here?* As I mentioned earlier, theologically I had been taught that there were no kids in heaven. So I asked the angel, "Where did all these children come from?"

"These are children that the earth did not want," he said. "God brought them here."

"But I thought people went to heaven because they chose to go."

"No, Jesse, children must be taught the oracles of God."

I saw that many people were teaching those kids, so I realized that God was using people as well as angels to teach others in heaven about Him.

Then I asked, "Are you talking about abortions?"

He said, "Yes. These children can't wait to see their mothers."

The ages of the children I saw seemed to be from about three to ten years. Babies were off in another place.

Jesus Appeared to the Children

The people had been shouting joyfully and those little children were playing beautiful songs on their harps and singing. They were all excited. Then I heard a whispering. The people in gowns were looking toward the city. People around me began saying, "He's coming! He's coming! He's coming!"

I asked the angel, "Who's coming?"

"You shall see the Holy One," he said.

All of a sudden, I saw a Light coming out of the city, but it was far from me. The children ran toward the Light. I knew then that it was Jesus!

I couldn't see His face because I was too far away. All I could see were His hands reaching out to the kids as they played and sang and hugged Him. Those kids adored Him. Then I heard Him say,

Suffer the little children to come unto me...for of such is the kingdom of God (Mark 10:14).

As We Got Closer to the City

Then the angel said to me, "We must go to the city."

As we were walking in that direction, the angel said, "You're going to get weaker and weaker." He had kept fruit for me and offered it to me frequently.

I noticed some of the people in gowns who were slipping out from under those trees and walking toward the city. They almost got there; then they stopped, turned around and had to go back. It seemed as if they were depressed.

I heard someone say, "There is no depression here. Just eat of the Tree of Life, smell the leaves for healing and let your spirit grow. You shall stand at the Throne of God."

Then I saw people who were wearing those robes of righteousness just marching into the city.

I Made It to the City!

As we walked up to the city, we came to the jasper wall described in the book of Revelation. That wall is huge! According to Revelation 21:17 (AMP), the wall is **144 cubits, (about 72 yards).** We don't know whether that is the height or the thickness. But the city is **12,000 stadia (about 1,500 miles); its length and width and height are the same** (v. 16 AMP). I wanted to see the names on the foundations of that wall described in Revelation chapter 21 which says:

> **And the wall of the city had twelve foundations, and in them the names of the twelve apostles of the Lamb...**
>
> **And the building of the wall of it was of jasper: and the city was pure gold, like unto clear glass.**
>
> **And the foundations of the wall of the city were garnished with all manner of precious stones...**
>
> **And I saw no temple therein: for the Lord God Almighty and the Lamb are the temple of it.**
>
> **And the city had no need of the sun, neither of the moon, to shine in it: for the glory of God did lighten it, and the Lamb is the light thereof.**
>
> **Revelation 21:14,18,19,22,23**

The angel started inside, but I said, "Stop! I've read about this. I want to see the names of the apostles."

So I looked at the pillars. The first name I saw on the foundations of heaven was Peter. I thought the second name would be John, but it was Paul. The names I saw listed were Peter, Paul, James and John. I just started shouting with joy because I was so excited to see those names which I had studied.

The angel said, "Come quickly. You must have your appointment."

But I wanted to see all those names. I said, "I can preach about this on the earth. Let me get all these names in order in my mind."

But the angel took me by the hand and said, "Come." So we got back into our chariot and went into the city.

Right inside the city I saw the Book of Life. It is huge, about five feet five inches vertically and one and one-half inches thick. It looked like it is bound in a gold lamé cloth. It has an inscription in it, etched in deeply. There were people standing around it, but I don't know what they were doing. The angel wouldn't let me stop there.

As we were going down the streets, I saw a man with a crown on his head, who I later discovered was David. I said to the angel, "Stop. Who is this?"

He said, "You shall meet him shortly." Then we passed him by.

Seeing Jesus for Myself

All of a sudden, the angel stopped our chariot and said, "Kneel. He's here."

I felt weak then and fell to my knees. The angel handed me some fruit and said, "Eat this." So I did.

As Jesus walked toward me, those children ran up to Him. They sang praises to Him, and He just hugged them. As the kids sang, He rejoiced with them.

To me, He looked like a shaft of light. He was so glorious!

He turned toward me, and I fell at His feet.

I said, reverently, "Oh, God!"

He said, "I'm here."

As I was kneeling down, I noticed Jesus' feet looked like burnished brass. I thought there would be scars in His hands and feet. But it wasn't like He had been cut and scarred. I could see the holes in His feet. They were so big — about the size of a nickel —

that light was shining through them. I realized then just how big the nails were that had been pounded into His feet and hands at His crucifixion.

We don't realize how much Jesus suffered on the cross. There are no adjectives to describe what He really went through.

He put His hand on my shoulder and said, "Jesse, stand to your feet."

I stood and looked at Him. There was a brilliance coming out of Him that seemed like waves of glory. The light was emanating from Him. His clothes were beautiful and looked like solid diamonds that were sparkling.

Jesus was taller than I thought He would be. I would guess Him to be from five feet eleven inches to six feet one inch.

I thought at first His hair was white; but when He turned His head, I caught a glance and saw that it was light brown. When He looked at me, the glory of God was emanating from Him.

I said, "Jesus!"

He said simply, "Do you like this place?"

I said, "Yes, Sir."

"Tell My People I'm Coming"

The first thing I thought of doing was confessing my sins to Him. I said to Him, "I'm not the man I should be, I've made some mistakes." When you get to heaven, all you want to do is repent!

But He said, "You're forgiven. I made a plan of redemption."

"Then what am I doing here? Why are You doing this?"

"I want you to go back and tell My people I'm coming."

"But they won't believe me," I said.

"They didn't believe it for centuries, but I came, and I am coming again."

Then He put His hand on my shoulder. I'll never forget it. He looked at me and said, "There are many things you shall see and learn here, but I have brought you here so that you will go tell My people I'm coming."

I said, "They know that."

"No, they don't know that. I brought you here so that you would go tell them I'm coming. Do you hear Me? I'm coming. Go tell them."

You may ask, "What does Jesus look like?"

Jesus is beautiful — not just handsome, but beautiful. When I looked into Him, I saw love and kindness. He is love. He can look right through a person. Glory is emanating from Him. His eyes are like pools of love and He is the color of light.

As you reach out to hug Him, there's an automatic reaction: He just grabs you. He can be looking at millions of people, yet you're the only one He sees.

Then I said, "You took care of all those babies, didn't You?"

"I never lose any of them," He said.

Sometimes a thought would come into my mind, and before I could speak it, He would answer me.

In my mind I thought, *I bet You're mad at some of those people.*

In response, He said, "No, I forgive them, for they know not what they do. But many have come to the knowledge of Who I am and they shall share their life and eternity with the gift I sent to the earth." He spoke as if the Father were speaking through Him.

While talking with Jesus, I could see the great compassion that He has for those who haven't received Him as their Savior. He asked me to tell you that He's coming again soon!

I guess that's why I haven't rested in my life. There was such an urgency in His Voice. We must know something is up. Jesus is coming soon!

Maybe you're wanting to see Jesus, to see heaven, to look at its flowers and walk on its streets of gold. Maybe you want to see the city with that glorious, magnificent skyline. Our natural mind can't comprehend what God has for us. That's why we need a new body: so that we will be able to consume what God has for us.

That's why I want to tell everyone I meet to accept the fact that Jesus died in their place so that their sins would be forgiven. I have seen heaven and know what is waiting for everyone there. That's why I want to see people trusting Jesus as the Lord of their life and enjoying the blessings that the Father has for them.

CHAPTER EIGHT

Lessons From Heaven

Jesus put His arm around me as He watched a man walking toward us who was wearing a crown. Then He said to me, "I want you to meet another king."

I recognized him as the man that I had seen earlier. He had reddish hair and a red beard. I knew immediately it was David. As he approached us, he spoke to Jesus, "To the great King of kings I bow."

Jesus said, "Jesse, I want you to meet the king of Israel." The Lord said, "Take Jesse to his home. Show him what I have prepared for him. Then bring him to My Throne. I must go. My Father wants Me." Then He turned and walked off.

I looked at the man Jesus had introduced and said, "Hello." I didn't know what else to say. "Your name is David, isn't it?"

He answered, "Yes."

Bowing down, I said, "Oh, king!"

"Don't bow to me," he said. "You just looked at the King of kings. I've been assigned to take you around."

I asked, "Is there anything I can do for you?"

He replied, "You don't understand; we're servants here. We're here to serve you. What do you want, Jesse? What do you need?"

I looked again for shadows around the angel. He asked, "What are you looking for?"

I said, "You don't have a shadow." (I was still amazed by the fact that there was no darkness whatsoever. None! It's all light! That amazed me.)

The angel looked at me and explained as he had before, "No, there are no shadows here. God is Light, in Whom there is no darkness, nor shadow of turning."

Then David said, "I've been instructed by the Lord to take you to your house."

"My place?" I said. I wanted to stay at the jasper wall. I wanted to talk more to Abraham and to Jesus. I was interested in that angel. I wanted to look at those gold streets and smell all the flowers. But there was a schedule to keep.

Paul Was Still Teaching the Oracles of God

David took me into a house — I don't know who it belonged to. We walked into a beautiful foyer and by the wall in the corner I saw the Apostle Paul sitting with several men. I can't tell you about the house because my eyes were on Paul. He and the men were discussing the Word of God. Paul was short! I noticed as he was sitting on the bench that his feet didn't touch the ground. He looked up at us and said, "Jesse!"

I said, "He knows my name!"

Paul asked, "Jesse, what are they saying about my gospel?" (He still calls it *his* gospel.)

I said, "Man, I preach everything you said. Everything! If you came back, you could get me for copyright infringement. I do, I preach everything you said. The Pauline epistles are wonderful!"

He smiled at me. I wanted to talk to him for a long time. He is still a teacher, and I sensed that Paul knew of deeper revelations that we will enjoy learning once we are in heaven. I was attracted to Paul's knowledge. He's still explaining and teaching others about God.

I said to Paul, "You were caught up in the third heaven. I read in the Scriptures that you were caught up." I was thinking of 2 Corinthians 12:2: **I knew a man in Christ above fourteen years ago, (whether in the body, I cannot tell; or whether out of the body, I cannot tell: God knoweth;) such an one caught up to the third heaven.**

"Just like you," he interrupted.

"Yeah, this is a wonderful place!" I said.

Paul agreed saying, "I spent my whole life to be here."

I had so much to say to him. I told him, "I think you are the greatest intellectual mind that was ever drawn to Christianity."

"Thank you," he said. "The Lord has been gracious to me."

He was so humble! His humility ministered to me. I guess if I had a hero in the Scripture, it would be the Apostle Paul. He kept the faith in spite of great afflictions. He was born into a family of prominence;

he was conscientious of social law and was a Pharisee in the tribe of Benjamin. He was climbing an ambitious ladder, but when he met Jesus, he went as high as a man can climb. He kept the faith, fought a good fight and finished the race. I am also determined to fight a good fight like Paul. I want it to be said of me, "He kept the faith." And I have done that. I don't say that arrogantly because we all can make a decision and set ourselves on a course to do something we've determined to do.

I said to Paul, "You went through great persecution."

"Yes," he answered, "but I kept the faith. I focused my life on faith. That's how you get things done."

The next statement he made is one I have used in sermons. He said, "Our affliction is but for a moment. People have made it a lifetime. Change it back to a moment."

I get goose bumps when I think about that! It's a moment, not a lifetime. "Change it back to a moment," he told me. I have used Paul's statement in seminars and people compliment me for the message, but that word didn't come from me. It came from Paul. Look at how Paul said it in 2 Corinthians 4:17,18:

For our light affliction, which is but for a moment, worketh for us a far more exceeding and eternal weight of glory;

While we look not at the things which are seen, but at the things which are not seen: for the things which are seen are temporal; but the things which are not seen are eternal.

Paul continued to speak to me, "Change it back to a moment, Jesse." Then he whispered, "Change it back to a moment. Don't leave it a lifetime. I've kept the faith, and that's how it's done. And it worked."

I'll never forget Paul's words for as long as I live. All the troubles I have had since that trip to heaven in 1988 just roll off my back.

Then he smiled at me and said, "Never change the message because of the hearers. Speak what God gives you."

I wrote those words down when I came back so that I wouldn't forget what he said to me. I was able to speak with him awhile longer before David and the angel told me to keep moving toward our appointment. I will share more of what Paul said to me in a later chapter. David seemed to want to let me take my time, but the angel kept reminding me that I had more places I needed to go.

David Talks About God's Answers

As David walked along with me, I said to him, "You've always been an interesting character to me. I was prophesied to as a child that I would have a life similar to yours."

He laughed and said, "You've got some things ahead!" I laughed, too.

I told David that I was a musician. He seemed to light up because music is his gift.

"Of course, I haven't written songs like you have," I added. David laughed again. I felt like I had known him all my life. His personality was strong and commanding. But he was a servant because of the work that God has done in him. He seemed like a friend, yet he was a king. He was the only one I saw with a crown on his head other than Jesus.

He had an awe about him, and great respect was shown to him by the people who walked by. He had an infectious smile. Now I've had people tell me that I have pretty teeth, but his teeth are beautiful. He had a hardy laugh. He shook when he laughed. I felt so comfortable with him.

I asked him how he got his ideas for his songs because I know that musicians get ideas from all kinds of creative ways.

"From the Lord," he answered. We both laughed again.

He continued, "I did write songs of my experiences, like a lot of other people do. But the better ones are when I allowed the lordship of God in me to come out more than the trouble that I spoke about."

He didn't say this, but I knew that he meant that some people picked up his trouble as something they had to go through, too. But what he was saying was that when he allowed God to come through him, he was able to write anointed messages like, **The Lord is my shepherd; I shall not want.**

He did use Psalm 23 as an example as he explained, "I allowed God and the anointing to come through in that song. In other songs I sang strongly about my troubles. I think I should have allowed more of the answer to come through, instead of the complaining." Those weren't his exact words, but I knew that was what he meant.

Then he added, "I wish I had written more songs about God's answers than about my problems. If I had listened to the Lord, there are some things I would have never gone through. Now you have my record, so follow the record God told me and you won't walk through some of the places I walked through."

I'll never forget those words.

He asked me what instrument I played and I said the guitar and the piano. "The piano is like the harp," I explained because I didn't think they had pianos in David's days.

"I know," David replied. I laughed because I realized that he knew much more than I did about everything, but I didn't stop asking questions that seemed to have obvious answers.

I Saw My House in Heaven

Then he took me to my house. When I walked up, I looked at the grounds. There was a water fountain in the front yard and manicured grass. It was the prettiest place I had ever laid eyes on. I said, "This is my house?"

"Yes," David said. "Would you like to go inside?"

"Yes, I want to go inside!"

To me, the foyer of a home sets the mood of a house. When I went through the front door, there were tall ceilings and crown moldings.

"Do you like it?" David asked.

"Yes, I like it. This is beautiful!" Everything was decorated and the furniture was just the kind I liked. I said, "This place is beautiful! I wasn't expecting to see this. Just look at this place! Hey, I have furniture like that on the earth! I love this!"

"Yes, the Lord knew you would like it, so we put it in your home. We told you He would give you the desires of your heart," David said. "All desires are met here. Everything has been thought of — all your desires and some that you could not even think of."

Everything was perfect down to the last detail! It was all so beautiful! I looked at more physical things in my home than anywhere else. There was marble, and there was a table in the foyer with golden eagles on it! I said, "Look at this!"

"David," I said, "there are lots of things here that look like things on the earth."

"Well, the earth is the Lord's taste," he answered. "Remember, He created it. So a lot of what you see there you will see here. Come, let me show you more."

"The thing that bothers me, David, is that I never thought there would be things here like mountains."

"Jesse, the earth is God's creation. His taste there is His taste here. Every desire you could possibly think of has been met to your specification for your home, plus God put a few of His own. Let me show you more."

Families Are Reunited

As we were leaving the house to go on to the Throne room, I saw a man, a woman and some kids outside. I walked to the door and said, "Who are they?"

"This is a family that was killed in an airplane accident," David said. "They all are here."

I was puzzled. "I need to ask a question. Excuse me for my ignorance, but I didn't think we lived together as families. One woman told me she didn't want to go to heaven if she couldn't live with her husband. I have a wife named Cathy. Are we going to be together?"

"Yes, you live together," he answered. "But not as you know it on earth. It's better than you think."

So I asked the family, "Where are all of you going?"

They said, "We're going to our house and then on a picnic. Would you like to come?"

I said, "Yes!" I really wanted to go with them on their picnic.

Then David stopped me saying, "We must go to the Throne first. Then we will take you that way. I have been commissioned to bring you to the Throne. That I must do. The best is yet to be seen. We must go quickly." He wanted to show me more houses on our way to the Throne.

I Saw Where the Prophets Lived

He took me down a street that looked similar to Old New York City, or St. Charles Street in New Orleans, where the beautiful block mansions were.

"Whose houses are these?" I asked. "The patriarchs'?"

"Yes," he said, "these are where the prophets live."

I saw their homes, and I saw some of the prophets we know from the Old Testament books.

As we went by, they waved and said, "Hi, David."

When I waved back, they said, "Hi, Jesse."

I said, "They know me?"

David explained, "You have preached their sermons. God blesses them with knowing their messages are still reaching people. They like it because God used them so much that their sermon material is still going on."

I had to keep eating more of that copper-colored type of fruit because I felt weak. It was sweet tasting and very juicy, and it gave me strength.

Jonah Teaches of the Nature of God

I had seen Jonah earlier, but the angel was constantly moving me toward that appointment I had. But on the street where the prophets live I recognized Jonah again as he was coming from his house. I was so interested in knowing about that whale that swallowed him. I wanted to know if it was a fish or a whale and what it had been like to be in the belly of a fish for three days and three nights.

I rushed up to him and said, "Boy, you were in that whale! How was it being in that fish?"

It seemed to me that he hesitated, as though he felt discontentment just for a second. I felt that maybe I had brought an unpleasant event to his memory he had been allowed to forget.

Then Jonah corrected me. He said, "No, I was in *disobedience.*"

"Disobedience," I repeated, realizing I had focused on the wrong part of the story.

I remembered how God told Jonah to go to the city of Nineveh and proclaim that their attention on worthless idols was causing them to forsake God — their Source of mercy and lovingkindness. Chapter 4, verse 2, of the book of Jonah shows how Jonah sensed that God would revoke His sentence against them, and he ran from God's assignment.

While on a ship headed in the opposite direction from Nineveh, a great storm rose up and the mariners cast lots to see whose fault it was that the evil had come against them. The lot fell on Jonah. After questioning him, they tossed him overboard! The storm stopped immediately. When the mariners saw that, they worshipped Jonah's mighty God! A great fish, or some Bible versions say a sea monster, swallowed Jonah. Jonah was in the belly of the fish for three days and three nights. (Jonah 1:1-17.) But I could see now that Jonah wasn't concerned so much about the fish during those three days; he was concerned about his disobedience to God.

"Disobedience is a powerful thing against you. Not only in the life that you live now, but here."

I still don't quite understand what Jonah meant by that statement, but he majored on the point of disobedience. I think he meant that disobedience causes a delay in reaching the level we could reach. We may reach the level in eternity, but I believe that obedience to God's Word moves us more quickly to the level that God has planned for us.

I remember his exact words to me. He said, "God's Word must be followed to the letter."

Jonah continued, "When I came out of there, I had one thing on my mind, and that was to do what

God had told me to do. But when God kept the city, instead of wiping it out, I felt irritated about that."

I was trying to grasp every word of what he was saying. I knew that Jonah had prophesied to the people of Nineveh that God was planning to overthrow the city in forty days. The people believed Jonah, and the king proclaimed a fast to begin penitent mourning for their sins. Neither man nor beast tasted anything, nor drank water to show their sorrow. The king pleaded, **Who can tell, God may turn and revoke His sentence against us [when we have met His terms], and turn away from His fierce anger so that we perish not** (Jonah 3:9 AMP).

Chapter 3, verse 10, records, **And God saw their works, that they turned from their evil way; and God repented of the evil, that he had said that he would do unto them; and he did it not.** Chapter 4 shows that Jonah knew that God was gracious and merciful, slow to anger, and of great kindness. But because God is merciful and didn't back up Jonah's promise that the people of Nineveh would be overthrown, Jonah wanted to run again. I guess we could say he pouted.

Then Jonah said to me, "I felt irritated because I thought of myself more than I thought of the nature of God. His nature is not to destroy, but to heal and to bless."

I was given so much to think about. I wanted to see more of the city, but I didn't have staying on my mind. I knew I had a destiny or something to fulfill. I knew God was letting me see heaven for a specific reason. The angel gave me more fruit and led me toward the Throne of God.

CHAPTER NINE

I Saw God's Throne

I felt weaker and weaker as we approached the Throne room. It looked to me like millions of people were there. Looking around, I saw twenty-four empty seats near the Throne. I said, "I've read in the Scriptures about the twenty-four elders." (Revelation 4:4.) "Those are their seats! Where are they?"

"Jesse, we're servants here," David told me as he had earlier. "They're out in the city and in Paradise blessing and helping people. We help people here. Everyone serves. Somebody is always trying to do something for you. Someone will always ask, 'What can I do for you?'"

Even the flowers turn toward you in an attitude of service. They turn and "look" at you. They don't have eyes, but they know you're there. And you can't smash them; they go through your legs. I would look down at a flower I had stepped on and think, *Why didn't I smash it?* You can't kill anything there. There's no destruction.

After seeing the way everyone served each other in heaven, I don't think God is looking for brilliant individualists. I believe He's looking for team players. I remembered the account in the Bible when James and John, the sons of Zebedee, asked Jesus how they could have a special place in heaven. In Mark 10:43-45 Jesus explains:

...but whosoever will be great among you, shall be your minister:

And whosoever of you will be the chiefest, shall be servant of all.

For even the Son of man came not to be ministered unto, but to minister, and to give his life a ransom for many.

Angels Were Praising God

There were several big angels with wings flying around the room. They were huge! Their faces were distinctive as though carefully chiseled. They looked like they had a thirty-foot wing span. The angel with me didn't have wings; he looked just like a human being.

The closer I got to the Throne of God, the weaker I became, because of the glory of God. When people are coming to the Throne, you see God's anointing on them, that glory on them, from the different levels. But when you get to the Throne, nothing compares to the glory of God.

When the light from the Throne hit me I couldn't stand up; I fell down, and the angel gave me more of the fruit saying, "Eat this so you can withstand the glory of God." I ate it, but my knees had just buckled. I stayed on the floor. Everyone else was standing up. For a lack of a better way of putting it, when you stand or fall at the Throne, God's glory washes out your glory. His glory goes in you and on you.

Everything in heaven is beautiful. The floor looked like marble with gold in it, gold threads or veins running through the marble. Although I couldn't look up for very long at a time, I looked up from the floor in the direction of the overwhelming Light, and I saw Him! I saw Elohim, Jehovah God, Yahweh sitting on the Throne! But I saw His feet — only His feet. The Light was so bright that came from Him, I couldn't see His face. Now I know why the Scripture says we can't see Jehovah's face and live — at least, I knew I couldn't! I had to keep looking down, the Light was so intense. But I looked again, and I saw the lower part of His hand resting on the arm of the Throne. He is so big — you can't describe Him in a dimension. His hand is huge! His body, the form of it, is sort of like energy, spirit. There's a wall around the Throne, but the Throne is higher than the wall — that's why you can see the Throne from every direction, from a distance. And that power, that energy-like smoke of God, covers all around the chair of the Throne itself.

I heard a sound, *Whoooooosh!* There was a massive amount of energy in that place. That's the only way I can explain it. It was God's power! You hear that noise, then the energy goes back into Him. There is smoke and power and noise — the place is noisy! And angels are hollering.

The angels with wings were circling the Throne, singing and shouting, "The Great God Jehovah!" Every time they circled the Throne they praised God because they saw a new facet of Him they had never seen before. And they express what they see by saying "Holy! Holy! Holy!" That's how vast God is! Even though the angels have been flying around

God's Throne since the beginning of their existence, they are still seeing new revelations of His character, His love and His glory!

There was a cloud that looked like smoke going up from the Throne and I heard that massive sound, *Whoosh!* It was power like I've never experienced in my life. Then I saw God's finger barely move and when it moved, an angel that was flying near Him was thrown up against a wall. *Bam!* It didn't hurt the angel, but I felt if God just barely moved, a universe could be annihilated.

Jesus Preached With Power!

I was still lying on my face and getting weaker. In that mass of energy and power I could see God, Jehovah — His feet — sitting. There is a huge platform in front of the Throne like a stage. It seemed level to me, but actually it was raised. Everything in heaven is raised. The topography of the land goes up toward the Throne. Then out of that massive energy of Light and love and power I saw Jesus come in human form. There He was, like I had seen Him in Paradise. What seemed to be millions of people at the Throne of God fell down before Him.

For the first time in my life, I could understand the Trinity in physical terms. Jesus came out of the cloud and the power of the Father. Jesus literally came out of the very existence of Jehovah God, and when He did, the people shouted. Jesus and the Father were One, yet They were Two. He was in the Father and the Father was in Him. He was at the right hand of God. When He came out of that power, He was in human form — something we could touch.

All my life as a minister, I thought of Jesus as a teacher, a mild-mannered, calm person. When He came out onto the platform of that Throne, I could hear a sound from the Father, *Whoosh! Whoosh!* It was the sound of power! The Jesus I heard that day was not a teacher, even though obviously He can teach; He was a dynamic preacher.

I had always thought of Jesus as being a quiet teacher, but He was full of power and preached with authority. All the people there were listening. Jesus preached with great emotion. I could see that He was torn with compassion for those who were still on earth.

Jesus preached of His coming to earth. He said, "I am going to get My Body, and My Body shall reside

in this place that My Father has created for us all."
There was a stirring among the people, and they
began shouting and praising God.

He began to shout: "I'm going to get your
brothers! I'm going to get your sisters! I'm going to
get your family! I'm bringing them back to this place
to live with Me forever and ever!" He was a preacher
full of victory, shouting and hollering! He was
excited, and the people were screaming and
hollering, too.

As He preached, people — even though they were
in new celestial bodies — fell under the power of
God. Even in heavenly bodies they fell under God's
power!

Then I heard Jehovah's Voice, saying, "I am well-
pleased."

I was lying on the floor, trying to take in all that
was happening. It was the most amazing, powerful
experience I have ever gone through.

I couldn't look at Jehovah's face, but I could look
at Jesus. You see, the heart of God is the Father; the
face of the Father is unveiled by the Son, Jesus; the
Voice of God is heard through the Holy Ghost; the
Hand of God is laid open through the Church.

As Jesus was preaching, I saw Him turn around several times and look into that massive light. But I realized that I couldn't do that. I had to keep looking down, but I could look up long enough to see glimpses of what was around me, and I could see Jesus' face. I could hardly bear the Father's power. Jesus would look back at the Father, sometimes just looking over His shoulder, as if they didn't want to be separated even by sight very long. I could sense the love of God in Jesus, and I could see the affection and love flowing back and forth between the Father and the Son. I had never before seen love like that. It seemed magnetic.

Jesus would walk in and out of the power, the fire, that massive amount of energy. When Jesus walked back into the energy, as He got closer, I would have to put my head down again, because I couldn't handle the Light. But that form of a Man as He walked toward that energy would transform back into Spirit.

I understood how the Trinity are Three, yet They are One. Still lying on the floor, I turned my head toward that angel and asked, "Where's the Holy Spirit?"

"He is on the earth," he said.

Of course! Later when I thought back to the incident, I felt so stupid to have asked such a dumb question at the Throne of God. I'm still embarrassed about it.

I Saw Children in the Thoughts of God

I saw new lives of little babies singing and flying around God's Throne. It seemed to me that babies just came out of the breath of God. They looked like they were wearing nightgowns. They flew into the presence of Jehovah.

I realized they were new souls who came from the thoughts of God. God thinks kids. Now I know why those newborn babies are so precious. Babies are gifts given to us directly from the Throne of God.

I heard them saying to God, "Can I be a spirit? Would You send me to the earth so I can be a spirit? I want to be a redeemed person. Can I be a spirit?" And while I watched, I heard that mighty sound of God's power, *Whooosh!* I saw these babies leave the Throne by the power of God.

I don't know how long I was there, but I felt that I couldn't stand it much longer. That's why I think that I was there in the flesh — that my body was physically there.

Suddenly, the angel said, "We must go. It's too strong for you. Come." So he took me out from the Throne, and David walked with us.

I got back into the chariot with David and the angel. As we were leaving, people were waving at me.

I asked David, "Will we see Abraham before we leave?"

"Yes," he said, "you will see him before you go back."

People began going out from the Throne, back into the city and into Paradise. They were helping other people and being a blessing to them. I saw people discussing theological points about the Word of God among themselves.

We went back down that street of the prophets. As we passed a beautiful building, I asked, "May I go in there?"

"No," the angel answered. "No human eye has seen inside this building."

"What is it?"

"That is to remain in the knowledge of Jehovah. No human eye has seen it, not even Enoch."

I have no idea what it was.

Then I Saw Jesus Again

As we were going down that street of the prophets, all of a sudden I heard that familiar Voice saying, "Jesse." I turned around. It was Jesus.

I said, "That was a great message. It was wonderful."

He was gleaming as He said, "It is a true message. That's why you were sent here. You are to tell My people."

I said, "They won't believe me."

His Voice was firm, "You just tell them. When they think it not, so shall I come."

Then He said firmly, "Go tell My people I'm coming."

My destiny was for this lesson. I thought, *That's it? That's why He brought me here?* I was disappointed to learn that my trip to heaven was for this lesson. I thought I was going to learn something nobody had ever heard. My purpose for going to heaven was to hear Jesus say that He's coming back for us, and I am to tell others.

I must have had unbelief written all over my face. I said, "Lord, they know that."

And He became stern with me and raised His Voice as He said, "No, they don't! You go tell them I'm coming."

Paul wrote to us concerning the return of Christ in 1 Thessalonians 4:13-18 (NIV):

Brothers, we do not want you to be ignorant about those who fall asleep, or to grieve like the rest of men, who have no hope. We believe that Jesus died and rose again and so we believe that God will bring with Jesus those who have fallen asleep in him. According to the Lord's own word, we tell you that we who are still alive, who are left till the coming of the Lord, will certainly not precede those who have fallen asleep.

For the Lord himself will come down from heaven, with a loud command, with the voice of the archangel and with the trumpet call of God, and the dead in Christ will rise

first. After that, we who are still alive and are left will be caught up together with them in the clouds to meet the Lord in the air. And so we will be with the Lord forever. Therefore encourage each other with these words.

The intensity of His love for us was evident in His face and Voice. When I looked into His eyes, I understood the importance of what He was saying. At that instant, I knew His coming is the greatest thing we can wait for. The message that Jesus is coming soon is the greatest news we can share!

CHAPTER TEN

God Will Wipe
Away All Tears

Jesus had just revealed His heart's desire to me. He asked me to tell others that He's coming back to earth. He was filled with compassion and was waiting for me to respond to Him.

I said, "Lord, I'll do everything I know to do. I love You with all of my being. But I've made some mistakes in my life."

He said, "I don't know that you did. I washed them away. You're free."

"Thank You!" I said.

I saw tears well up in His eyes as He made the next statement to me. He said, "The worst day of My life is yet to come." Then suddenly the Father was speaking through the Lord Jesus Christ — God —

was sharing with His creation. He said, "You know that Scripture where I said I will wipe away all tears in heaven?"

"You know, Lord, I've never truly understood that," I replied. I knew that John spoke of God's plan to remove all tears in Revelation 21:1-5:

And I saw a new heaven and a new earth: for the first heaven and the first earth were passed away; and there was no more sea.

And I John saw the holy city, new Jerusalem, coming down from God out of heaven, prepared as a bride adorned for her husband.

And I heard a great voice out of heaven saying, Behold, the tabernacle of God is with men, and he will dwell with them, and they shall be his people, and God himself shall be with them, and be their God.

And God shall wipe away all tears from their eyes; and there shall be no more death, neither sorrow, nor crying, neither shall there be any more pain: for the former things are passed away.

And he that sat upon the throne said, Behold, I make all things new. And he said unto me, Write: for these words are true and faithful.

Now Jesus was explaining this mystery to me saying, "Those include the tears in My eyes, Jesse. On that great Judgment Day, I will have to tell some of the creation I love to depart from Me. I dread that day. I dread it! I dread it!"

He had tears in His eyes when He was saying this. It touched my heart. We always focus on God wiping tears from our eyes. We do not understand the love that God has for us. I wanted to reach out to Him and comfort Him, so I put my hand on the Lord. I didn't know what else to do. I could tell that Jesus was hurting.

There were other times in Scripture that we knew Jesus cried. When He wept for Jerusalem he could change the situation. We saw His tears for Lazarus, but He raised Lazarus from the dead. We saw His tears at the crucifixion, but He changed that memory with His resurrection. But once the judgment comes, He can't change it. His Word will be final. When He has to turn man away, His most prized possession, He can't change it back. He dreads that day.

Then He said, "Jesse, it's final. I can't change it. Tears flowed from My eyes the day My creation, Adam, fell. But I knew I would send Myself. I had a chance to touch people. But that day is coming, and it's final. Once it's said, I can't change it. I have to wipe the tears from My eyes."

The Lord was firm with me, "Tell them I'm coming, Jesse."

I said, "Lord, when are You coming back?"

He didn't answer me directly but He said, "Everyone looks for the signs when they ought to look for My witness."

I understood Him to mean that we are looking at the signs of the times as the return of the Lord. He wants us to look at the witness of Who He is, the Person of Jesus Christ.

I realized that He didn't know when He was coming in terms of the day and year. But I see that His coming is not just His return, it is the witness of Who He is. When He said in the gospels that His kingdom was not of this world, He was trying to get the people to see the witness of Who He is and not just understand the signs that pointed to Him as the Messiah. I felt that He was saying our eyes should be on Him, Jesus, instead of on the great tribulation period.

But as His Body, we are in disobedience by fighting each other. We're not coming together with the witness of Who He is. Satan's greatest ally is our division in the Body of Christ. I think Jesus wants us, the Church, to be looking more at Who He is instead of focusing on our differences.

If the Body of Christ, the Church, would begin to reveal Who Christ is, and lift Him — the Person of Jesus Christ — up for the world to see, people will be drawn to Him. I think we can delay His coming by waiting for a sign before we act on His Word instead of showing the witness of Who He is to a world of lost and dying people.

Many of us think that miracles get everybody to come to church. But miracles actually create doubt. John the Baptist didn't have a single miracle in his ministry, yet he caused moral reform. I think he's the only preacher who ever had the church come out to see him. Even the biggest heathen in town, Herod, had respect for him.

We need to preach Jesus, the Person, and Christ, the message of His anointing. People don't understand Jesus as a Person. I know Him as a Person. I didn't get that knowledge in heaven; I got it that night in Boston, Massachusetts, when I got saved. I believe if the Church worked together to show the world a witness of Who Jesus is, and if we would preach the message of Christ, we could evangelize the world in a day.

Jesus couldn't tell me when He is coming. I could see why the Father hadn't revealed to Jesus when that day of judgment will be. I felt Jesus would have told me if He had known the day, so we could all be prepared. I don't think He could keep that secret because His love for mankind is so strong. Mark 13 speaks of signs that precede the return of the Lord. Verses 32-37 say:

> **But of that day and that hour knoweth no man, no, *not the angels which are in heaven, neither the Son, but the Father*.**
>
> **Take ye heed, watch and pray: for ye know not when the time is.**
>
> **For the Son of man is as a man taking a far journey, who left his house, and gave authority to his servants, and to every man**

his work, and commanded the porter to watch.

Watch ye therefore: for ye know not when the master of the house cometh, at even, or at midnight, or at the cockcrowing, or in the morning:

Lest coming suddenly he find you sleeping.

And what I say unto you I say unto all, Watch.

I realized that God deeply desires our love. I didn't know before how much He needed me to reach out to other people. I have always thought of how much I need Him, not how much He needs me.

I said, "I'll do anything for You. I know that may be a rash statement; Peter said it. But as far as I know, I would do anything for You."

He smiled at me and said, "I chose you. No one else wanted you, and I need you, Jesse."

I said, "Okay. I'll tell every soul I meet that You're coming."

He said, "I brought you here for this." Then He said, "Now you must go back."

"I would like to stay here," I said.

"You shall be here for eternity," He said. Then He looked at David and the angel. "David, Jesse likes mountains. Take him by way of the mountains."

He looked at me and smiled, and I noticed His features again. I couldn't tell what color His eyes were, but they looked like pools of love. He said, "I'll see you soon. One day we'll never part. It will be forever, and sooner than you think."

Isaiah prophesied of God's promise to wipe away tears in Isaiah 25:8.

He will swallow up death in victory; and the Lord God will wipe away tears from off all faces; and the rebuke of his people shall he take away from off all the earth: for the Lord hath spoken it.

John learned the same lesson when he saw heaven. Revelation 7:17 records:

For the Lamb which is in the midst of the throne shall feed them, and shall lead them unto living fountains of waters: and God shall wipe away all tears from their eyes.

I could see the compassion in Jesus' eyes. He doesn't want to anyone to perish, but wants all to come to repentance so they will receive all that the Father has for them.

A Trip Into the Mountains

I got back into that chariot-like machine with David and the angel. Jesus had told them to take me by the mountains on my way home. As we went past the mountains, I could hear the children singing. I cannot explain how wonderful heaven is. I can only agree with Paul's words in 1 Corinthians 2:9,10:

But as it is written, Eye hath not seen, nor ear heard, *neither have entered into the heart of man, the things which God hath prepared for them that love him.*

But God hath revealed them unto us by his Spirit: **for the Spirit searcheth all things, yea, the deep things of God.**

When we were near the mountains, I saw people having picnics — just eating and enjoying themselves. Then I saw the family I had talked with before. One of them said to me, "Sorry you can't stay. But when you come, we'll eat together."

I saw little apartments and condominiums. I asked David, "What are these things?"

He said, "Jesse, every desire is given here. Every one of the people who live there have a home in the city but some of them like a place in the country, too. Not only do people live in the city, some like apartments as well as their homes, so the great God has provided it. Every desire of an individual is met here."

I said, "Do you mean to tell me that people with mansions decided they wanted a place out here?"

He says, "Yes. Would you like one? It shall be done, because the great God is merciful. Every desire is met." I didn't hear a sign of greed in this. The Lord was just blessing the people.

Psalm 37:3,4 confirms:

Trust in the Lord, and do good; so shalt thou dwell in the land, and verily thou shalt be fed.

Delight thyself also in the Lord; and he shall give thee the desires of thine heart.

I saw people of many different races there. Then I noticed a group of Oriental children being taught the oracles of God by a lady. I asked, "Are their parents here?"

"Some are," David said, "but most of them are not. They come to an age when they have to accept or reject God. The parents may reject God and go the other way, but the great God is merciful; He doesn't reject their children. Sometimes children pass away at an early age, so we teach them and they grow."

I knew parents who had recently lost a baby would be happy to know that they would meet their child here. Their child will be taught the oracles of God.

I believe that if people could see the treasures that God has stored up for them in heaven, they wouldn't have such a hard time understanding God's will to prosper and heal them while they are on earth. There are leaves for healing in heaven, and prosperity is everywhere. Anything that you can think of, anything you could want on earth has already been given to you there.

Mankind has a difficult time receiving what God has for us because sin has touched us. Sin still steals things from us by stealing our thoughts and confidence in God's promises.

Have you ever noticed the word "gospel" is only in the New Testament? That's because *gospel* means "good news," and there isn't any good news in the Old Testament. Before Christ died for us, it was "do or die." The Old Testament only shows us the law that we cannot keep. But Christ was bruised for our iniquities and by His stripes we are healed! By His grace we can approach the throne of God and be reconciled to the Father and to His glorious plan to bless us.

If you have ever wanted to do something for the Lord, you can tell someone that He is coming and that He wants to come for them. Help Him reach those who haven't heard His Good News.

As I was leaving Paradise, Abraham said, "I shall see you again."

Looking back at him, I felt like I could hardly wait for that day when like the beggar in Luke 16, verse 22, I will be **carried by the angels into Abraham's bosom.**

I said, "Thank you." Then I was on my way home again.

CHAPTER ELEVEN

Back Home Again

That chariot began to accelerate. I heard its power — *Whoosh!* Within seconds of leaving Paradise, I was back in my room and in the same position as when I had left at 1:00 p.m. In my mind, everything seemed to go so fast. I thought I had been gone for about thirty minutes, but it was 6:15 p.m. when I looked at the clock again. I had been in heaven five hours and fifteen minutes!

Someone was supposed to pick me up for church at 6:45 p.m., so I dressed in a hurry. I was still befuddled and I thought, *I'm not saying anything about this. People will think I'm crazy.*

The man who had been picking me up every night for those meetings was usually a talker. But this time while driving to church, he didn't say a word; he just kept looking at me. I thought, *Did I say something to offend him?*

When we got there, the service had already started. They were singing, so I walked up to the front of the church. People began pointing their fingers at me, saying, "Look at Brother Jesse. He's shining." There was a light on my face. I had been in the presence of the glory of God.

When I walked to the platform, the pastor just backed up. I was going to sit in the little pew, but he motioned for me to come. I said to them, "I have been in the presence of God." But they thought I meant I had been praying.

Knowing they didn't understand, I explained, "No, I'm not talking about praying; I'm talking about being in God's physical presence."

I had been to heaven!

I didn't even preach that night. I didn't say anything, but people began falling under the power of God's Spirit! There was ministry throughout the auditorium without me saying any more.

The Goodness of God Passed Before the People

Moses couldn't look at the face of God and live, but God let him look at His glory. Putting Moses upon the rock and hiding him in the cleft of it, God covered Moses with His hand until His goodness passed by. Look at Exodus 33:18-23:

And he [Moses] said, I beseech thee, show me thy glory.

And he said, I will make all my goodness pass before thee, and I will proclaim the name of the Lord before thee; and will be gracious to whom I will be gracious, and will shew mercy on whom I will show mercy.

And he said, Thou canst not see my face: for there shall no man see me, and live.

And the Lord said, Behold, there is a place by me, and thou shalt stand upon a rock:

And it shall come to pass, while my glory passeth by, that I will put thee in a clift of the rock, and will cover thee with my hand while I pass by:

And I will take away mine hand, and thou shalt see my back parts: but my face shall not be seen.

When Moses came down from Mount Sinai after seeing the goodness of God and receiving God's instructions for Israel, the Bible says in Exodus

34:29 that he was not aware that his face was radiant because he had spoken with the Lord. People tell me that my face shines when I talk about my trip to heaven. I can't see that, but I know how refreshed I feel whenever I talk about it or ponder the messages I received while I was there.

I'm not trying to compare myself with Moses; I'm just saying that God is still the same today! Seeing God's glory just makes me cheerful! That's why I feel called to a ministry of cheerfulness.

God still puts us upon a rock and hides us in the cleft of it so that we can stand in the presence of His goodness. That rock is Jesus Christ. We are covered with the blood of Christ so that we can stand in God's goodness today, just like Moses did on Mt. Sinai.

He Gives Us Living Water

When the children of Israel needed water, God gave them a rock and living water flowed from it whenever they needed it. First Corinthians 10:4 explains where that water came from:

And [they] did all drink the same spiritual drink: for they drank of that spiritual Rock that followed them: and that Rock was Christ.

When I was in heaven, I felt dehydrated like you are (if you're a motorcycle rider) after being on a motorcycle all day long in heat. Your body can start trembling when you get that dry. I was given water from the River of Life at least five times. It tasted like cold water and it quenched my thirst. I was so refreshed when I drank that water. The fruit sustained me, too, but at the Throne of God I drank water again and felt wonderfully refreshed.

Jesus told the woman at the well that she should ask Him for water in John 4:10,14:

Jesus answered and said unto her, If thou knewest the gift of God, and who it is that saith to thee, Give me to drink; thou wouldest have asked of him, and he would have given thee living water...

But whosoever drinketh of the water that I shall give him shall never thirst; but the water that I shall give him shall be in him a well of water springing up into everlasting life.

I believe that God wants a refreshing revival of joy in His Church. I don't care how mature you are, you're still God's child. I believe that God wants to revive His people with the refreshment of His goodness, as a father plays with his children, so our Father in heaven enjoys hearing our laughter and joy.

God isn't looking for only a serious relationship with us. God doesn't want us to be scared that we will have our hand slapped for doing something wrong. I believe there are times for holy awe, or silence. But I believe that God would like to see joy restored to the Church. Nehemiah said in chapter 8, verse 10, **the joy of the Lord is your strength.**

When our joy is restored, perhaps we will look for ways to work together with our brothers and sisters in other denominations, instead of competing or fighting with one another as so often happens. The greatest enemy to the Body of Christ is the friendly fire of people speaking against people.

This message of heaven can cross all denominations because we all want to go to heaven. To most people heaven is a place. Since I've been there, to me heaven is God. It's where He dwells. It's His house. As we believers are all here on earth on our way to being with God in heaven, we can learn how to work together to bring the witness of Jesus into the world.

As we testify of God's goodness, more people will be drawn to Him. As we show people how to receive Jesus, He will fill them with living water, so that they will be refreshed in the goodness of God. Revival displays God's glory.

The Mystery of God's Plan Is Revealed

Paul explained the mystery of God's will for us in Ephesians 1:3-10 (AMP):

May blessing (praise, laudation, and eulogy) be to the God and Father of our Lord Jesus Christ (the Messiah) Who has blessed us in Christ with every spiritual (given by the Holy Spirit) blessing in the heavenly realm!

Even as [in His love] *He chose us [actually picked us out for Himself as His own]* in Christ before the foundation of the world, *that we should be holy (consecrated and set apart for Him) blameless in his sight, even above reproach, before Him in love.*

For He foreordained us (destined us, planned in love for us) to be adopted (revealed) as His own children through

Jesus Christ, in accordance with the purpose of His will [because it pleased Him and was His kind intent]—

[So that we might be] to the praise and the commendation of His glorious grace (favor and mercy), which He so freely bestowed on us in the Beloved.

In Him we have redemption (deliverance and salvation) through His blood, the remission (forgiveness) of our offenses (shortcomings and trespasses), in accordance with the riches and the generosity of His gracious favor,

Which He lavished upon us in every kind of wisdom and understanding (practical insight and prudence),

Making known to us the mystery (secret) of His will (of His plan, of His purpose). [And it is this:] In accordance with His good pleasure (His merciful intention) which He had previously purposed and set forth in Him,

[He planned] for the maturity of the times and the climax of the ages to unify all

things and head them up and consummate them in Christ, [both] things in heaven and things on the earth.

In verses 17 through 20 of this first chapter of Paul's letter to the Ephesians, Paul prayed that God would grant them insight into God's mysteries so that they would understand the greatness of God's power in and for those who believe as He demonstrated when He raised Christ from the dead. What Paul prayed for the Ephesians is also for us as believers today.

[For I always pray to] the God of our Lord Jesus Christ, the Father of glory, that He may grant you a spirit of wisdom and revelation [of insight into mysteries and secrets] in the [deep and intimate] knowledge of Him,

By having the eyes of your heart flooded with light, so that you can know and understand the hope to which He has called you, and how rich is His glorious inheritance in the saints (His set-apart ones),

And [so that you can know and understand] what is the immeasurable and unlimited and surpassing greatness of His power in and for us who believe, as demonstrated in the working of His mighty strength,

Which He exerted in Christ when He raised Him from the dead and seated Him at His [own] right hand in the heavenly [places].

I have seen this goodness and power of God and desire to share this Good News with everyone. I have to admit it took a long time before I could tell anyone what I had seen.

A Message To Share: Jesus Is Coming!

I didn't tell Cathy about my experience in heaven until five days later. I said, "Cathy, sit down. I want you to listen to this." Then Cathy's sister, Deborah, and her husband came over.

I was about ready to tell all of them about my experience when Deborah interrupted me, saying, "You know, I had a dream the other night that I was in heaven, sitting with my four children. But I realized that I must have misunderstood my dream because I only have three children."

Then I looked at her and said, "No, you have four. You miscarried a baby, remember?" Then I said to them, "Grab your chairs and listen to this."

When I told about seeing those children in heaven, Deborah burst out crying. I said, "What you dreamed was true: you have four kids. Your other one is waiting for you in heaven."

Deborah was so blessed and touched by knowing that I had seen children in heaven who were waiting for their parents to arrive.

Maybe you or someone you know is looking forward to seeing a child who was taken to heaven. Though you cannot bring the child back (see 2 Samuel 12:22,23), you can go to your child by trusting Jesus as your Savior.

Live a Life That Glorifies God

Don't bill me as "the man who went to heaven." God called me to be an evangelist and to preach the Gospel. You don't have to believe my testimony, but it literally happened.

Now I know what Jesus looks like, and I know what waits for those who believe in Him. Receiving a revelation of truth doesn't give a person the power to live a holy life. We each have to walk out our salvation and depend on the Holy Spirit to give us the power to overcome sin and live like Christ wants us to live.

What I am saying is, God has given me the gift to *preach* this book. But He hasn't given me the gift to live it. I have to work out my salvation with fear and trembling. Some people think that because there is a great call on their life, they automatically have the gift to live it, but that isn't true. They still have to take God's Word and obey it, and apply it to their lives.

I don't take this lightly. I'm not interested in the spectacular; I'm interested in the supernatural. I find the spectacular brings glory to man; the supernatural brings glory to God. If you want a movement to flow in the anointing of God, and then to continue, never let your ministry get over into the spectacular; keep it in the supernatural where God's power is the only force working.

Isaiah proclaimed in chapter 2, verse 11, that arrogant men will be humbled and the pride of men brought low, that the Lord alone will be exalted in that day. God's glory is spectacular enough without man adding to it.

People tried to call attention to the spectacular moments in Jesus' ministry. They would say, "Oh, You great Miracle Worker!" But He said, "It's not Me but My Father in Me Who doeth the works. I have come to do the will of My Father" (John 14:10; 5:30 author's paraphrase.)

As the Church, we are the hand of God reaching out to a dying world. We must live as His children and share a testimony of His power to save us from our sins so that others will see the witness of His power in our lives.

Take my word for it: Jesus is coming, and He told me to tell His people. I've seen heaven, it is a real place more beautiful that you can imagine. You don't want to miss out on heaven! And you don't want others to miss it either!

CHAPTER TWELVE

Everyone Was a Team Player in Heaven

When I tell people about my trip to heaven, I am surprised by the peace it brings to their lives. Prior to writing this book, I had only told excerpts of my visit while ministering in a few places. After sharing my story, people told me that hearing about heaven put joy in their hearts. Some said that they have been to heaven and have seen the very places I described. Others say they understand the Trinity better and that they feel closer to God.

I kept quiet about it for so long, but the Lord prompted me that it was time to tell you what I saw. Many publishers asked me to write a book, but I wouldn't even consider it. It's difficult to explain how dear this story is to me. I couldn't imagine how to go about telling you what I saw.

One morning, when I was at a ministers' conference, the Lord spoke to me, "I want you to do this in book form."

Seven years had passed since my trip to heaven, and God was telling me it was time to tell the story. I asked the Lord, "How am I going to do this?"

That day, Buddy Harrison, my publisher, came up to me, put his hand on my shoulder and gently said, "Jesse, I don't want to push you, in any way, shape or form, but I think you need to put your story in a book." I knew it was confirmation of what the Lord had said to me that very morning.

The trip to heaven was so special to me, I have never wanted anyone to try to analyze or evaluate it. Some people may think that I would tell the story to make money from selling the book. I would use the money for the gospel anyway. But this story is a part of me. It changed me. I now realize I didn't see heaven just for me. The stories will help other people, too.

I can still hear Paul's voice saying, "Change it back to a moment. Change it back to a moment." He wanted me to remind you that our afflictions and hardships are not for a lifetime. They are just for a moment compared to eternity. He said:

For all things are for your sakes, that the abundant grace might through the thanksgiving of many redound to the glory of God.

For which cause we faint not; but though our outward man perish, yet the inward man is renewed day by day.

For our light affliction, which is but for a moment, worketh for us a far more exceeding and eternal weight of glory.

2 Corinthians 4:15–17

Verse 17 is the one that has been taken out of context for centuries. Paul said, *Our light affliction, which is but for a moment.* Our affliction is for a moment. Not a lifetime. If you're not careful, the church will make your moment become a lifetime. There's a vast difference between a moment and a lifetime.

Religion has caused the Body of Christ great pain through this verse. The first thing I was told after I got saved and went to church was, "It's gonna be rough all the days of your life, Jesse. The devil's gonna stomp you and beat you, but he who endures till the end shall be saved."

They took a moment of hassle and made it a lifetime.

You don't have to wait a lifetime to be healed! By His stripes you *were* healed. (1 Peter 2:24.) Many people have frustrated God's grace by taking a moment and stretching it into a lifetime.

Would you like to take your lifetime of misery and change it back to a moment of light affliction? A radical and energetic conviction changes a lifetime back into a moment. It requires one small word. One word. The devil's afraid of it. Every government in the world is afraid of it. People are afraid of it.

It's called, "NO!"

Communism threatened, "We'll hold you."

Russia stood up and said, "NO!"

Foundations start to crack when you tell the devil, "No!" Jesus didn't just tell Satan, "No!" He went further and said, **Get thee behind me** (Luke 4:8). In other words, "Get back; you make the landscape disgusting."

I think when Jesus died on the cross, Satan and his followers were rejoicing at their victory. All the while Jesus whispered, "It ain't over till it's over!" (author's paraphrase.)

Now, whenever something tries to discourage me, I hear those words, "Change it back to a moment."

When the doctors said I was dealing with a sickness, I heard, "Change it back to a moment."

When I was frustrated with details in our television ministry, I heard Paul say, "Change it back to a moment."

As soon as my attitude changed, God spoke to me and told me what to do with the ministry. The frustration fled. So I am compelled to do whatever I have to do to help you understand that Good News of heaven.

The message from heaven is, "The struggles in this life are only temporary, they are only a moment compared to eternity. Don't let it last a lifetime! Change it back to a moment."

God Needs Us To Tell Others

We, the Church, are the hand of the Lord. It is through us that others find out how much God loves them. It never occurred to me before that the Lord *needs* us, but we are His plan to reach others.

When I saw the tears in Jesus' eyes as He thought about having to turn away those who rejected Him, I felt changed. I have a new compassion for others. I want to help others understand His great love for them.

Before my trip to heaven, I was critical and full of judgment toward others. I judged the personality behind the ministry, but I've learned that God works through personalities. Some of us may be loud and others quiet. God uses our differences to reach different people. I'm not as critical since I have seen God's love. It's a physical substance that rubs off on you, and after you see it you walk in more mercy and grace.

Since I saw Abraham and David so eager to serve others, I want to be like that, too. I want to be a servant of the Lord. I want to help you to see how much the Father loves you. I want to help people receive all the glorious riches that God has stored up for them. I have a new compassion for the Body of Christ.

Everyone was a team player in heaven. There were only two distinctions — those in gowns and those in robes. The ones in robes were serving the ones in gowns. All the people in robes were helping the ones in gowns to understand the oracles of God so they could go on into the Throne and stand in the presence of the Father.

I believe I saw the garments of salvation and the robes of righteousness that Isaiah spoke of in chapter 61:10. He said,

I will greatly rejoice in the Lord, my soul shall be joyful in my God; for he hath clothed me with the garments of salvation, he hath covered me with the robe of righteousness, as a bridegroom decketh himself with ornaments, and as a bride adorneth herself with her jewels.

I don't understand church splits. I don't understand jealousy from preachers. In heaven, we all receive the blessings of God. On earth, only God should be exalted! I don't have to be in the forefront. I'm on a team. I'm going to get the Super Bowl ring, too, even if I'm sitting on the bench. I may not be a first-stringer; but it doesn't matter — I will still earn the team ring. God needs His believers to be team players.

I asked Paul To Tell Me His Secret

When I was with Paul in heaven, I was so excited to be with a man who did so much to teach us about God's will for our lives. I'm an information man and I have wondered about Paul's family. He was a Sanhedrin, so some people say he was married.

"Can I ask you a question?" I inquired.

"Yes," he answered.

"Some people said you had a son. Were you married?"

Paul smiled and looked straight at me. I'll never forget his words as he said, "What I would rather give people is my life, my life's work. I'm a dead man, Jesse." He continued, "The reason why you don't know much about me and my personal life, is because it wouldn't help anybody."

I listened closely, as Paul explained, "And if you notice, you don't know much about Jesus' personal life, because it really doesn't help anybody. It's His work that we need to know."

Looking back, I see how funny it was for me to have thought Paul was going to tell me he had a wife and two kids. We don't even know what happened to Jesus between the age of twelve and thirty years. Whatever happened was not relevant to our lives or it would have been written down. Others who have truly given their lives to the Lord have very little recorded about their personal lives.

Paul reminded me, "It isn't them that liveth, but Christ that liveth in them."

After that conversation, David told me I had to leave. I turned around and thanked Paul, "I appreciate your time."

He clenched his hand into a fist and said, "Preach this gospel. Preach this gospel!" It was obvious that he was stirred. His voice was strong and bold.

"I will preach this gospel."

"That's why you're here," Paul confirmed.

David interrupted us and said we had to move on. I can still hear Paul telling me to "preach this gospel." Preaching is my life. If I can't preach in a church, I preach it to myself. People laugh when I tell them that I preach my own revivals to myself. More than anything I think about completing my destiny. My mind never rests; I'm a driven man.

I've got boldness, too. I'm not embarrassed to preach the gospel and tell people about heaven. We died with Christ to the basic principles of this world. Dead people can't get embarrassed. In the Scripture below Paul was writing to the Colossians, but it's to all believers. I know it's talking to me, and it's talking to you, too. Consider his point about being dead to things in this world.

> **Since you died with Christ to the basic principles of this world, why, as though you still belonged to it, do you submit to its rules....**

> **Since, then, you have been raised with Christ, set your hearts on things above, where Christ is seated at the right hand of God. Set your minds on things above, not on earthly things. For you died, and your life is now hidden with Christ in God. When Christ, who is your life, appears, then you also will appear with him in glory.**

> **Colossians 2:20; 3:1-4 NIV**

The Church Is the Hand of the Lord

The Body of Christ is the hand of the Lord. God reaches others through us. I'm not just trying to promote my own ministry, because if that's the case, I could have been on a lot more television stations with the money I have given away to other ministries. But if I see someone further along in promoting the gospel through an avenue that it might take me one or two years to build, I would rather give them money to do more of what they are doing. I understand how the Body of Christ must work together to evangelize the world.

I've learned that I can't carry the responsibility of all I see to be done alone — we are to be team players here in our work for the Lord. When I see other people proclaiming the gospel, I want to support them.

You can run yourself to the point that God could still use you, but there's nothing left to use. I think that's one of the traps of Satan for someone not to complete their ministry. If Satan can't *stop* us, he will *push* us until we are so tired and weak that if we don't go to heaven right away, all we'll want to do is go there as soon as we can! Where we hurt the devil is on the earth. He would like to get us off the planet. Satan would rather have us in heaven than making trouble for him here on the earth.

A young preacher gave me a word of knowledge one time. He said, "Brother Jesse, the devil can't defeat you — you just run over him. So since he can't get in front of you and stop you anymore, he gets behind you and pushes. He says, 'Come on, man, come on! You've got to keep doing the work of God. Come on, Jesse! What are you going to sleep for, man? You could have taken that afternoon prayer session. Come on! Come on! Come on!' He's now behind you pushing. And you may not complete what the Lord wants you to do."

That hit me like a ton of bricks because it was a true word. It isn't part of my nature to rest much. And no matter how much I've pushed myself, the Lord still has given me the ability to finish what I'm doing. There have been times when I've walked out on that platform and been so tired I've said to Him, "God, I'm going to need some help here or I'm not going to last three minutes." And He says, "This anointing has saved you, and I will give it to you again." But see, that's disobedience. I think I will lose rewards for that because I'm not taking better care of myself.

The statement that inspired me a long time ago, "I would rather wear out than rust out," is still true, but I've learned that being obedient to the Lord means to rest sometimes and support others when I can. God even sent that angel to me one time to tell me to get some sleep! Matthew 11:30 tells us the Lord said, **My yoke is easy, and my burden is light.** When we are obedient to do what God tells us to do and not what *we* think we should do, we will be doing our part as one of the many members of the Body of Christ, and His burden will be light. I would always rather be preaching the gospel instead of resting! But to be obedient I make myself say *no* sometimes.

Now I'm not saying don't step out in faith! As I said before, I'm a man who believes in stepping out in faith — I jump out of that boat and walk on that water knowing that Jesus will keep me up if I start to sink. It's important to step out in faith! But what I'm saying is: Spend time with the Lord, and listen to Him. Take time to hear what He's telling you to do, and do that — what *He* tells you. The point is to listen to Him and obey. Then you'll live a rich and full life fulfilling the plan He has for you in the Body of Christ as His hand to reach others for Him.

Jonah Majored on Obedience

Jonah emphasized that it is important to follow God's words exactly. Rules for holy living are explained in Colossians 3 and believers are told to put to death whatever belongs to our earthly nature: sexual immorality, impurity, lust, evil desires and greed, which is idolatry. Because of these things that holy anger of God is coming upon the sons of disobedience. (v. 6 NIV.)

It's difficult for me to consider God's anger after seeing His great love, but He must come as He has promised, and we are told to rid ourselves of anger, rage, bad feelings toward others, curses and slander, and foulmouthed abuse and shameful utterances from our lips! (v. 8 AMP.)

Verses 9-14 (NIV) describe what I believe the patriarchs were wanting us to understand.

Do not lie to each other, since you have taken off your old self with its practices and have put on the new self, *which is being renewed in knowledge in the image of its Creator.* **Here there is no Greek or Jew, circumcised or uncircumcised, barbarian, Scythian, slave or free, but Christ is all, and is in all.**

Therefore, as God's chosen people, holy and dearly loved, clothe yourselves with compassion, kindness, humility, gentleness and patience. Bear with each other and forgive whatever grievances you may have against one another. Forgive as the Lord forgave you. And over all these virtues put on love, which binds them all together in perfect unity.

I guess I could say, as Paul did in Philippians 3:12, **I am apprehended of Christ Jesus.** *Apprehended,* according to Strong's Concordance, is taken from the word meaning "to take eagerly, i.e., seize, possess." It also means to "attain, come upon, comprehend, find, obtain, perceive, (over-)take."[1]

Not as though I had already attained, either were already perfect: but I follow after, if that I may apprehend that for which also I am apprehended of Christ Jesus.

Brethren, I count not myself to have apprehended: but this one thing I do,

---

[1] James Strong, "Greek Dictionary of the New Testament," in *Strong's Exhaustive Concordance of the Bible* (Nashville: Abingdon, 1890), p. 40, #2638.

forgetting those things which are behind, and reaching forth unto those things which are before,

I press toward the mark for the prize of the high calling of God in Christ Jesus.

Philippians 3:12-14

I have been apprehended, completely possessed with a Spirit — the Holy Spirit. I have been apprehended of Christ; I have been apprehended of His anointing. I have been seized by the Holy Spirit, and I am compelled by God's love and compassion to tell His people that Jesus is coming.

Conclusion

I wrote this book to give you a glimpse of heaven, to tell you how good and powerful God is, to tell you how much He wants to use that power to bless you, and to tell you of what I saw that will be waiting for us there — for those of us who believe in the Lord Jesus Christ.

In heaven I saw the great compassion Jesus has for those who haven't received Him as their Savior. If you haven't received Him as Savior, He loves you and wants you to spend eternity with Him so much that He took me to heaven to tell me to tell you He's coming soon.

The Lord is compassionate. He is willing and able to bless you. He wants to give you the abundant life here on earth. In the midst of those blessings, there will be afflictions — Psalm 34:19 says, **Many are the afflictions of the righteous,** but that verse also says, **the Lord *delivereth* him out of them *all*!** Jesus wants you to know from Paul's perspective that those afflictions are just for a moment.

The Lord will have blessings for you in heaven that you can only barely begin to comprehend now.

He wants to give you the desires of your heart. (Psalm 37:4.) He wants you to know that He is good.

The Bible says, **the goodness of God leadeth thee to repentance** (Romans 2:4). *Repentance* means asking the Lord to forgive you of your sins and believing that you are forgiven because Jesus died on the cross to take them for you. First Corinthians 15:3 tells us: **Christ died for our sins.**

When you understand how good God is, that He *is* love, you want to be with Him. The only way you can be with Him is by accepting Jesus by faith. Hebrews 11:6 says, **But without faith it is impossible to please him: for he that cometh to God must believe that he is, and that he is a rewarder of them that diligently seek him.** In John 14:6 Jesus said, **no man cometh unto the Father, but by me.**

If you don't know Jesus as your personal Lord and Savior, I would like to take this opportunity to introduce you to the greatest Friend you'll ever have. As you say these words, if you'll believe them with your heart you will be born again. (Romans 10:9,10.)

Prayer of Salvation

If you don't know Jesus as your personal Lord
and Savior, I would like to take this opportunity to
introduce you to the greatest *FRIEND* you'll ever have.
As you say these words, if you'll believe them with
your heart, you will be born again (Romans 10:9-10).

> *Jesus, come into my life. Forgive me
> of all my sins. I ask You to cleanse my
> heart, and make me a new person in
> You right now. I believe that You are
> the Son of God and that You died on
> the cross for me.*

> *Jesus, I want to thank You for loving
> me enough to die for me. I accept
> all that Your shed blood bought for
> me on the cross, and I receive You as
> my Savior and Lord. In Your name I
> pray. Amen.*

If you've just prayed this prayer, congratulations!
You are a "new creature in Christ" and, as
2 Corinthians 5:17 in the New Testament says,
*"...old things are passed away; behold, all things
are become new."*

Friend, you have a whole new life with Jesus to look
forward to starting now. Your slate is clean before
God. Your spirit has been reborn because of Christ's
great sacrifice and love for you. Please write and let
me know of your decision to follow Christ and I will
send you a free booklet to help you begin your new life
as a believer. So, write today and remember, Christ is
thinking about you and He only wants the best for your
life. God bless you!

Contact us on the web at:
www.jdm.org
or write to:
Jesse Duplantis Ministries
PO Box 1089
Destrehan, LA 70047

Heaven:

Selected Scripture References

Genesis 28:12:

> And he dreamed, and behold a ladder set up on the earth, and the top of it reached to heaven: and behold the angels of God ascending and descending on it.

2 Chronicles 18:18:

> Again he said, Therefore hear the word of the Lord; I saw the Lord sitting upon his throne, and all the host of heaven standing on his right hand and on his left.

Psalm 11:4:

> The Lord is in his holy temple, the Lord's throne is in heaven: his eyes behold, his eyelids try, the children of men.

Psalm 103:19,20:

> The Lord hath prepared his throne in the heavens; and his kingdom ruleth over all.

Bless the Lord, ye his angels, that excel in strength, that do his commandments, hearkening unto the voice of his word.

Isaiah 6:1-4,6:

In the year that king Uzziah died I saw also the Lord sitting upon a throne, high and lifted up, and his train filled the temple.

Above it stood the seraphims: each one had six wings; with twain he covered his face, and with twain he covered his feet, and with twain he did fly.

And one cried unto another, and said, Holy, holy, holy, is the Lord of hosts: the whole earth is full of his glory. And the posts of the door moved at the voice of him that cried, and the house was filled with smoke...

Then flew one of the seraphims unto me, having a live coal in his hand, which he had taken with the tongs from off the altar.

Ezekiel 1:1:

Now it came to pass in the thirtieth year, in the fourth month, in the fifth day of the month, as I was among the captives by the river of Chebar, that the heavens were opened, and I saw visions of God.

Daniel 7:9,10,13:

I beheld till the thrones were cast down, and the Ancient of days did sit, whose garment was white as snow, and the hair of his head like the pure wool: his throne was like the fiery flame, and his wheels as burning fire.

A fiery stream issued and came forth from before him: thousand thousands ministered unto him, and ten thousand times ten thousand stood before him: the judgment was set, and the books were opened...

I saw in the night visions, and, behold, one like the Son of man came with the clouds of heaven, and came to the Ancient of days, and they brought him near before him.

Luke 23:43:

And Jesus said unto him, Verily I say unto thee, To day shalt thou be with me in paradise.

John 1:51:

> And he saith unto him, Verily, verily, I say
> unto you, Hereafter ye shall see heaven
> open, and the angels of God ascending and
> descending upon the Son of man.

Acts 1:10,11:

> And while they looked stedfastly toward
> heaven as he went up, behold, two men stood
> by them in white apparel; Which also said, Ye
> men of Galilee, why stand ye gazing up into
> heaven? this same Jesus, which is taken up
> from you into heaven, shall so come in like
> manner as ye have seen him go into heaven.

Acts 7:55,56:

> But he, being full of the Holy Ghost, looked
> up stedfastly into heaven, and saw the glory
> of God, and Jesus standing on the right hand
> of God,
>
> And said, Behold, I see the heavens opened,
> and the Son of man standing on the right
> hand of God.

2 Corinthians 12:2-4:

> I knew a man in Christ above fourteen years
> ago, (whether in the body, I cannot tell; or

whether out of the body, I cannot tell: God knoweth;) such an one caught up to the third heaven.

And I knew such a man, (whether in the body, or out of the body, I cannot tell: God knoweth;)

How that he was caught up into paradise, and heard unspeakable words, which it is not lawful for a man to utter.

Revelation 2:7:

He that hath an ear, let him hear what the Spirit saith unto the churches; To him that overcometh will I give to eat of the tree of life, which is in the midst of the paradise of God.

Revelation 4:1:

After this I looked, and, behold, a door was opened in heaven: and the first voice which I heard was as it were of a trumpet talking with me; which said, Come up hither, and I will shew thee things which must be hereafter.

Revelation 7:9-17:

After this I beheld, and, lo, a great multitude, which no man could number, of all nations, and kindreds, and people, and tongues, stood before the throne, and before the Lamb, clothed with white robes, and palms in their hands; And cried with a loud voice, saying, Salvation to our God which sitteth upon the throne, and unto the Lamb.

And all the angels stood round about the throne, and about the elders and the four beasts, and fell before the throne on their faces, and worshipped God,

Saying, Amen: Blessing, and glory, and wisdom, and thanksgiving, and honour, and power, and might, be unto our God for ever and ever. Amen.

And one of the elders answered, saying unto me, What are these which are arrayed in white robes? and whence came they?

And I said unto him, Sir, thou knowest. And he said to me, These are they which came out of great tribulation, and have washed their robes, and made them white in the blood of the Lamb.

Therefore are they before the throne of God, and serve him day and night in his temple: and he that sitteth on the throne shall dwell among them.

They shall hunger no more, neither thirst any more; neither shall the sun light on them, nor any heat.

For the Lamb which is in the midst of the throne shall feed them, and shall lead them unto living fountains of waters: and God shall wipe away all tears from their eyes.

Revelation 19:11:

And I saw heaven opened, and behold a white horse; and he that sat upon him was called Faithful and True, and in righteousness he doth judge and make war.

Revelation 21:1-27:

And I saw a new heaven and a new earth: for the first heaven and the first earth were passed away; and there was no more sea.

And I John saw the holy city, new Jerusalem, coming down from God out of heaven, prepared as a bride adorned for her husband.

And I heard a great voice out of heaven saying, Behold, the tabernacle of God is with men, and he will dwell with them, and they shall be his people, and God himself shall be with them, and be their God.

And God shall wipe away all tears from their eyes; and there shall be no more death, neither sorrow, nor crying, neither shall there be any more pain: for the former things are passed away.

And he that sat upon the throne said, Behold, I make all things new. And he said unto me, Write: for these words are true and faithful.

And he said unto me, It is done. I am Alpha and Omega, the beginning and the end. I will give unto him that is athirst of the fountain of the water of life freely.

He that overcometh shall inherit all things; and I will be his God, and he shall be my son.

But the fearful, and unbelieving, and the abominable, and murderers, and whoremongers, and sorcerers, and idolaters, and all liars, shall have their part in the lake which burneth with fire and brimstone: which is the second death.

And there came unto me one of the seven angels which had the seven vials full of the seven last plagues, and talked with me, saying, Come hither, I will shew thee the bride, the Lamb's wife.

And he carried me away in the spirit to a great and high mountain, and shewed me that great city, the holy Jerusalem, descending out of heaven from God,

Having the glory of God: and her light was like unto a stone most precious, even like a jasper stone, clear as crystal;

And had a wall great and high, and had twelve gates, and at the gates twelve angels, and names written thereon, which are the names of the twelve tribes of the children of Israel:

On the east three gates; on the north three gates; on the south three gates; and on the west three gates.

And the wall of the city had twelve foundations, and in them the names of the twelve apostles of the Lamb.

And he that talked with me had a golden reed to measure the city, and the gates thereof, and the wall thereof.

And the city lieth foursquare, and the length is as large as the breadth: and he measured the city with the reed, twelve thousand furlongs. The length and the breadth and the height of it are equal.

And he measured the wall thereof, an hundred and forty and four cubits, according to the measure of a man, that is, of the angel.

And the building of the wall of it was of jasper: and the city was pure gold, like unto clear glass.

And the foundations of the wall of the city were garnished with all manner of precious stones. The first foundation was jasper; the second, sapphire; the third, a chalcedony; the fourth, an emerald;

The fifth, sardonyx; the sixth, sardius; the seventh, chrysolyte; the eighth, beryl; the ninth, a topaz; the tenth, a chrysoprasus; the eleventh, a jacinth; the twelfth, an amethyst.

And the twelve gates were twelve pearls: every several gate was of one pearl: and the street of the city was pure gold, as it were transparent glass.

And I saw no temple therein: for the Lord God Almighty and the Lamb are the temple of it.

And the city had no need of the sun, neither of the moon, to shine in it: for the glory of God did lighten it, and the Lamb is the light thereof.

And the nations of them which are saved shall walk in the light of it: and the kings of the earth do bring their glory and honour into it.

And the gates of it shall not be shut at all by day: for there shall be no night there.

And they shall bring the glory and honour of the nations into it.

And there shall in no wise enter into it any thing that defileth, neither whatsoever worketh abomination, or maketh a lie: but they which are written in the Lamb's book of life.

Revelation 22:1-21:

And he shewed me a pure river of water of life, clear as crystal, proceeding out of the throne of God and of the Lamb.

In the midst of the street of it, and on either side of the river, was there the tree of life, which bare twelve manner of fruits, and yielded her fruit every month: and the leaves of the tree were for the healing of the nations.

And there shall be no more curse: but the throne of God and of the Lamb shall be in it; and his servants shall serve him:

And they shall see his face; and his name shall be in their foreheads.

And there shall be no night there; and they need no candle, neither light of the sun; for the Lord God giveth them light: and they shall reign for ever and ever.

And he said unto me, These sayings are faithful and true: and the Lord God of the holy prophets sent his angel to shew unto his servants the things which must shortly be done.

Behold, I come quickly: blessed is he that keepeth the sayings of the prophecy of this book.

And I John saw these things, and heard them. And when I had heard and seen, I fell down to worship before the feet of the angel which shewed me these things.

Then saith he unto me, See thou do it not: for I am thy fellowservant, and of thy brethren the prophets, and of them which keep the sayings of this book: worship God.

And he saith unto me, Seal not the sayings of the prophecy of this book: for the time is at hand.

He that is unjust, let him be unjust still: and he which is filthy, let him be filthy still: and he that is righteous, let him be righteous still: and he that is holy, let him be holy still.

And, behold, I come quickly; and my reward is with me, to give every man according as his work shall be.

I am Alpha and Omega, the beginning and the end, the first and the last.

Blessed are they that do his commandments, that they may have right to the tree of life, and may enter in through the gates into the city.

For without are dogs, and sorcerers, and whoremongers, and murderers, and idolaters, and whosoever loveth and maketh a lie.

I Jesus have sent mine angel to testify unto you these things in the churches. I am the root and the offspring of David, and the bright and morning star.

And the Spirit and the bride say, Come. And let him that heareth say, Come. And let him that is athirst come. And whosoever will, let him take the water of life freely.

For I testify unto every man that heareth the words of the prophecy of this book, If any man shall add unto these things, God shall add unto him the plagues that are written in this book:

And if any man shall take away from the words of the book of this prophecy, God shall take away his part out of the book of life, and out of the holy city, and from the things which are written in this book.

He which testifieth these things saith, Surely I come quickly. Amen. Even so, come, Lord Jesus.

The grace of our Lord Jesus Christ be with you all. Amen.

Jesse Duplantis is a dynamic evangelist called to minister God's message of salvation through Jesus Christ to the world. From New Orleans, Louisiana, Jesse is anointed by God with a unique preaching ministry that melts even the hardest heart with hilarious illustrations and strong biblical teaching.

Since 1978, Jesse's primary goal has been to spread the Gospel. He has become a popular guest speaker at church meetings, conventions, seminars, Bible colleges, and on Christian television programs across America. His anointed sermons point sinners to Calvary and motivate Christians to exercise their authority over the devil by realizing their position in Christ.

Jesse believes that Christianity is not just something you talk about on Sunday; it is a day-to-day fellowship with the Lord Jesus Christ. It is this close fellowship with Jesus that makes the impossible suddenly possible.

Jesse's weekly thirty minute television program has touched millions of lives with the Gospel of Jesus. His program can be seen on over 2,700 television stations across the globe.

Through anointed biblical preaching, Jesse is bringing God's message of hope to our generation. A message that cuts through all denominational barriers, transcends human hypocrisy and frailty, and reaches the heart of mankind.

Look for these other books by
Jesse Duplantis

New! The Everyday Visionary

Wanting a God You Can Talk To
Also available in Braille

What in Hell Do You Want?

Jambalaya for the Soul
Also available in Braille

Breaking the Power of Natural Law
Also available in Braille

God Is Not Enough, He's Too Much!
Also available in Braille

The Ministry of Cheerfulness
Also available in Braille

Jesse's Mini-Books

Don't Be Affected by the World's Message
The Battle of Life
Running Toward Your Giant
Keep Your Foot on the Devil's Neck
One More Night With the Frogs
Leave It in the Hands of a Specialist
The Sovereignty of God
Understanding Salvation
Also available in Spanish

JESSE DUPLANTIS MINISTRIES
"Preaching the Gospel to the World."